THE CYPRESS HILLS

Fort Walsh has been dismantled and the police station moved to Maple Creek. Very likely at some future day admirers of ancient ruins will re-discover its desolate mud chimneys and entwine them with romances such as the poetry loving people of the east believe to be the lot of every man who preceded the CPR. *And possibly some policeman of "ye olden time," then a portly rancher or business man, with a double chin and a half dozen children, will visit the scene and, forgetting that the lot of a policeman is not a happy one, will chase his buffalo and fight his battles over again, telling of adventures in the imminent breach, of hair breadth escapes by flood and field, of balls in which the barracks were graced by the youth and beauty from all the neighbouring reserves, and altogether drawing the long bow with such a vengeance that the mud chimneys will wink at each other and grin horribly a ghastly smile.*

Edmonton Bulletin, August 18, 1883

The West does not need to explore its myths much further; it has already relied on them too long.

Wallace Stegner

Purich's Aboriginal Issues Series

THE CYPRESS HILLS

THE LAND AND ITS PEOPLE

Walter Hildebrandt and Brian Hubner

Purich Publishing
Saskatoon, Saskatchewan
Canada

96 97 5 4 3 2
Second printing

The publisher gratefully acknowledges the contribution of Parks Canada, Fort Walsh National Historic Site, towards the publication of this book.

Purich Publishing
P.O. Box 23032, Market Mall Postal Outlet
Saskatoon, SK Canada S7J 5H3

Canadian Cataloguing in Publication Data
Hildebrandt, Walter

    The Cypress Hills
    (Purich's aboriginal issues series)
    Includes bibliographical references and index.
    ISBN 1–895830–02–8

1. Cypress Hills (Alta. and Sask.) - History. 2. Indians of North America - Cypress Hills (Alta. and Sask.) - History. 3. Métis - Cypress Hills (Alta. and Sask.) - History. 4. Indians of North America - Cypress Hills (Alta. and Sask.) - Government relations - History. 5. Métis - Cypress Hills (Alta. and Sask.) - Government relations - History. I. Hubner, Brian, 1958– II. Title. III. Series.

FC3545.C9H83 1994   971.2403   C94–920025–5
F1079.C9H83 1994

Editing, design, and layout by Jane McHughen Publishing Services, Saskatoon
Cover design by NEXT Communications Inc., Saskatoon
Cover illustration by Ivan Eagletail
Maps by William Mills
Printed in Canada by Kromar Printing, Winnipeg
Printed on acid-free paper ∞

Outliers—rock outcroppings—such as those illustrated on the cover are common in the Cypress Hills area. They were used as vision quest sites, where young men would go to seek guidance. Ivan Eagletail is a Calgary artist and a member of the Tsuu T'ina First Nation.

CONTENTS

Readers will note that words like Aboriginal, Native, and Indigenous have been capitalized. In recent years, many Aboriginal people have argued that such words should be capitalized when referring to specific people, in the same manner that words such as European and American are capitalized. I agree; hence the capitalization.

Many First Nations have also decided to revert to their traditional names rather than continue to use translated versions of their names or the names given to them by government officials or missionaries. The authors and I are aware of this trend and support this change. However, so that this book could be easily understood by as wide a range of readers as possible, we have decided to use the names in common usage at the time the book was published, indicating the traditional names in parentheses following the first reference to a First Nation.

DONALD PURICH, PUBLISHER

FOREWORD

I was first contacted through my son, who works with Brian Hubner, to write a foreword for a book that he and Walter Hildebrandt were working on. I have had the opportunity to meet Brian at his workplace, Fort Walsh National Historic Site, a few times and have come to know him on a casual basis. I feel indebted to both authors for inviting me to be a part of their work.

At one time, the Cypress Hills were inhabited by four bands: Piapot, Lucky Man, Carry The Kettle, and Nekaneet. One of the Canadian government's policies involved the removal of the Native peoples from along the United States border, and this included the Cypress Hills.

The government, represented by the Indian agents, enlisted the aid of the North-West Mounted Police for this task. The removal came with varied reactions by each of the bands. When it came to the removal of Chief Nekaneet and his followers, the North-West Mounted Police did not force the band to leave. The Indian agent threatened to stop the treaty payments and rations promised to Nekaneet's people if they did not leave. Nekaneet knew that the Indian agent did not have a right to do this, nor did he have a right to say where Nekaneet and his followers were to live. He also knew that the Cypress Hills would help his people survive and prosper. It is through Nekaneet's knowledge and patience that his descendants still live within the Cypress Hills today.

My knowledge of the history of the Nekaneet Band comes not from research and reading, but from stories told by elders. The words that are being printed on this page are more my son's than they are mine. Just as those elders told these same stories to me, I am telling them to my son. Thank you.

GORDON OAKES
NEKANEET BAND ELDER

ACKNOWLEDGMENTS

This book is based on research I did for the Canadian Parks Service while working as an historian responsible for the history of Fort Walsh National Historic Site. I have rewritten and reshaped material that originally served program needs and was used by the guides interpreting the history of the Cypress Hills to the public at the fort and at Farwell's Trading Post.

Brian Hubner made valuable contributions both in research and writing. I met Brian as an enthusiastic guide some years ago. His dedicated search for material in repositories throughout Canada and the United States—particularly his interviews with ancestors of those who once lived and worked in the Cypress Hills—added greatly to this book.

I would like to thank the many colleagues I worked with during my years at the Canadian Parks Service from 1978 to 1992—the historians, archaeologists, planners, engineers, architects, interpreters, and administrators.

Over the years once, sometimes twice, a year, I would travel to the Cypress Hills to talk to the guides about the history of the site. I thank the guides I spoke with as we discussed an imbalance in the historical record that favored settler society and gave little space to the perspective of the Aboriginal people who lived in the Cypress Hills; together we began a process of inclusion that we must continue.

I dedicate this book to the guides at Fort Walsh and especially to Sarah, who was one of them.

WALTER HILDEBRANDT

I would like to acknowledge a very heartfelt debt of gratitude, first of all to my wife, Eileen, for her encouragement; to my mother, Freda, who typed an early version of this book into my computer, and finally to my father, Ed, who traveled with me on many of my trips to Montana and who first instilled in me a love of the history of the West.

BRIAN HUBNER

Both authors would like to thank those who assisted in the research for this book. In a project that stretched over a decade there were many archivists and librarians who were helpful in gathering photographs, books, and documents. Three descendants of the Cypress Hills traders were generous in sharing their personal records, photographs, and memories: George C. Lande of Pryor, Montana, a great-grandson of Abel Farwell; Leonard J. Hammond of Deer Lodge, Montana, grandson of George L. Hammond and Rosalie Wills; and Winniefred Eastlund Arhelger, great-granddaughter of Moses Solomon.

Thanks to the staff at the Glenbow, the Saskatchewan Archives, the Shortt Library, the Public Archives of Canada, the Provincial Archives of Manitoba, the Provincial Archives of Alberta, the Fort Assinniboine Preservation Association, the William K. Kohrs Memorial Library, the Historical Society of Minnesota, and the State Archives of Montana. Thanks to Bill Mills for drawing the maps and to George Melnyk and Jane McHughen for editing. Also special thanks to Joel Overholser, Donny White, Margaret Anne Kennedy, Lianne Roberts, Mimi Martin, Tom Kynman, Richard Stuart, and Julie Stafford.

Location of
Northwestern
Plains Nations
ca. 1820
over modern boundaries

The
Canadian-American
Northwest
ca. 1872

♦ Trading posts
▲ Whiskey trading posts
■ Military posts
● Civilian settlements

INTERNATIONAL BOUNDARY

NORTHWEST TERRITORIES

Last Mountain L.

Souris R.

Missouri Coteau

Missouri R.

Bismarck
Fort Abraham Lincoln
Northern Pacific R.R. (1872)

Old Fort Union (AFC)
Fort Buford

MONTANA TERRITORY
DAKOTA TERRITORY

Big Muddy Cr.

Missouri Coteau

Old Wives L.

Dirt Hills

Wood Mountain

Poplar R.

West Poplar R.

Rock Cr. (Porcupine Creek)

Yellowstone R.

Badlands

Powder R.

Vermilion Hills

Wood R.

South Saskatchewan R.

Old Chesterfield House (HBC)

The Great Sand Hills

Hand Hills

Red Deer R.

Ross Cr.

Swiftcurrent Cr.

East End (Chapel Coulee)

Pinto Horse Butte

Frenchman R. (Whitemud R.)

Milk R.

Fort Peck

Beaver Cr.

Tongue R.

Rosebud R.

Fort C.F. Smith (1866-68)

Little Big Horn R.

Big Horn R.

Cypress Hills
Battle Creek Métis
Head of the Mountain Solomon's Post
Farwell's Post

Battle Cr.

Fort Belknap

Bear's Paw Mtns.

Cow Island

Missouri River

Judith Mtns.

Lewistown

Musselshell R.

Clarke's Fork

Yellowstone R.

Bozeman Trail

Bow R.

Milk R.

Marias R.

Fort Benton Trail

St. Peter's Mission

Judith R.

Judith Basin

Diamond City

Missouri R.

Bozeman

Virginia City

Hand Hills

Sheep Creek

Old Bow River Fort (Piegan Post; HBC)

Fort Spitzee

Highwood R.

Willow Cr.

Belly R.

Fort Kipp
Fort Slide-Out
Fort Standoff

Oldman R.

Fort Whoop-Up (Fort Hamilton)

St. Mary's R.

Lee's Cr.

WHOOP-UP Trail

Sweet Grass Hills (Three Buttes)

Teton R.

Sun R.

Fort Benton

Fort Shaw

Helena

Butte

Bannack

Rocky Mountains

0   50   100   150 km
0   50   100 mi

wm

The
Canadian-American
Northwest
ca. 1882

■ Military &/or police posts
△ Fort Walsh outposts
● Civilian settlements

INTERNATIONAL BOUNDARY

0   50   100   150 km
0   50   100 mi

DISTRICT OF ALBERTA (1882); DISTRICT OF ASSINIBOIA (1882)

Treaty 4
(1874)

Treaty 6 (1876)

Treaty 7
(1877)

Last
Mountain L.
Vermilion Hills
Regina (1882)
Moose Jaw
(1882)
C.P.R. (1882-3)
Old Wives L.
Wood R.
Dirt Hills
Missouri Coteau
Souris R.
Missouri Coteau
Missouri R.

Saskatchewan R.
South Saskatchewan R.
Swift Current (1882)
Pinto Horse
Butte
East End
Maple Creek
Fort Walsh (1883)
Battle Cr.
Fort Walsh–Wood Mtn.–Fort Ellice Trail
Wood Mtn.
Big Muddy Cr.
Fort
Buford
Poplar R.
Yellowstone R.

Badlands

The Great
Sand Hills
Medicine Hat (1883)
Cypress Hills
Four-Mile Coulee
Ten-Mile Coulee
Kennedy's
Crossing
Frenchman R.
(Whitemud R.)
Fort Benton–
Fort Walsh Trail
Milk R.
Cow Island
Missouri R.
Judith Mtns.
Fort Maginnis
Lewistown

Red Deer R.
Bow R.
Blackfoot Crossing
Fort Calgary
(Calgary, 1883)

Fort Macleod–
Fort Walsh Trail
Lethbridge
Oldman R.
Belly R.

Milk R.
St. Mary's R.
Fort Macleod

Sweet
Grass Hills
Fort
Assiniboine
Loma
Marias R.
Teton R.
Fort Benton
Fort Benton–
Fort Macleod Trail
Sun R.
Great Falls
Missouri R.
Judith
Basin
Judith R.

MONTANA TERRITORY

Bear's Paw
Mountains

Rocky
Mountains
Missoula
Deer
Lodge
Helena
Butte
Fort Ellis

Park City
Billings
Clarke's Fork
Big Horn R.
Fort
Custer
Little
Big Horn R.
Fort
Keogh
Miles City
Tongue R.
Rosebud R.
Powder R.

Northern Pacific R.R. (1879-83)
Bismarck
Fort Abraham Lincoln

MONTANA TERRITORY
DAKOTA TERRITORY

wm

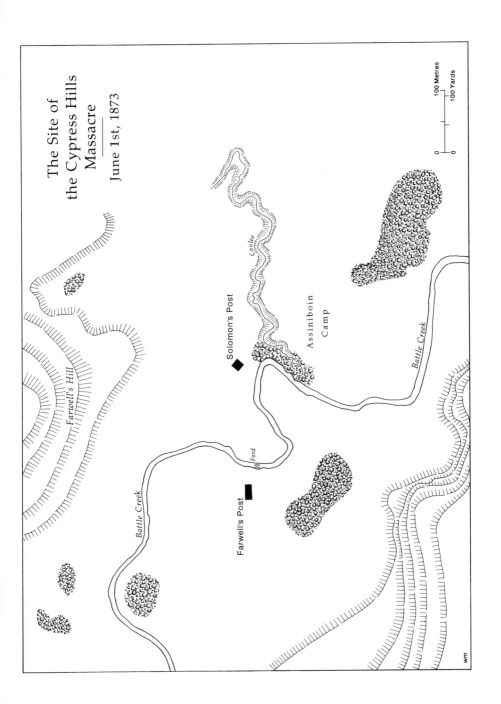

The Site of
the Cypress Hills
Massacre
June 1st, 1873

Farwell's Hill

Battle Creek

Coulee

Solomon's Post

Assiniboin
Camp

Battle Creek

Ford

Farwell's Post

100 Metres
100 Yards

0
0

wm

The
Cypress Hills

Above 3,500' (1067 m)
Above 4,000' (1219 m)

East Block

Centre Block

West Block

ALBERTA
SASKATCHEWAN

TRANS-CANADA HIGHWAY

Medicine Hat

Maple Creek

Irvine

Walsh

Fort Walsh

The Gap

CYPRESS HILLS
PROVINCIAL PARK

(WEST
BLOCK)

CYPRESS HILLS
PROVINCIAL PARK
(ELKWATER)

FORT WALSH
NATIONAL HISTORIC
SITE

East End

Cypress Lake

Head of the Mountain

Eagle Butte

Elkwater L.

Medicine Lodge Coulee

South Saskatchewan R.

Seven Persons Creek

Ross Creek

Gros Ventre Cr.

Bullshead Cr.

MacKay Cr.

Boxelder Creek

Maple Creek

Bone Cr.

Swiftcurrent Creek

Frenchman R.
(Whitemud River)

Battle Creek

Lodge Creek

Bare Creek

Manyberries Creek

0   10   20 km
0   10   20 mi

INTRODUCTION

The Canadian West was never a frontier waiting to be taken or conquered. For hundreds of years the Cypress Hills were a place of rich and varied flora and fauna that Aboriginal peoples of the prairies relied upon for their subsistence. They were a place of shelter where bands wintered as they moved off the open plains to avoid the biting western winds. The game in the Hills was plentiful in both summer and winter. In the forests of the Cypress Hills grew the long and narrow lodgepole pine so prized by all the Aboriginal peoples with access to the Hills. The poles manufactured from these trees were ideal for lodge poles and for both dog and horse travois.

For some of the Aboriginal peoples, this land—which had been by-passed by the glaciers that leveled the surrounding plains—was believed to be the place where the weather came from: "The Thunder Breeding Hills." Many plains people made their way to the Hills for food and shelter, and because they were believed to be a great spiritual place. The young came for vision quests to this strange outlier, climbing to the top of hills surrounded by deep forests with grand, awesome panoramas extending far out onto the prairies.

In the nineteenth century the Métis established wintering bases in the Hills. From the shelter of the Hills they pursued the diminishing buffalo herds that rarely came into Canadian territory after the 1870s. But the role of the Métis was still important—these Métis provisioners manufactured pemmican for the fur-trade posts in Western Canada. The Métis were followed by American free traders let loose into "Whoop-Up Country" to ply their whiskey trade across the western plains in the aftermath of their Civil War. These traders, who helped with the slaughter of the buffalo, were followed by Canada's Mounties, who came to make the West safe for the White settlers who would arrive in the wake of the Cypress Hills Massacre of 1873. Thus these mysterious and strange hills have had a long human history.

Traces of human life go back to arrowheads some five thousand years old and culminate in the cattle trails of the ranch country that makes up the most recent past. The process of history has left the hills strewn with artifacts of both man and nature: rock piles, bones, trails, burial sites, cellars, and fences. The Hills have been part of the full cycle of invasion, conquest, colonization, exploitation, development, and expansion that characterizes the market economies that dominate the world today.

This book is a record of the process of history, not its evolution. What has taken place in the Cypress Hills is not necessarily a progression of history; perhaps in our times we are witnessing more of a cycle of history than a linear advance. As agriculture declines on the prairies, the grasslands may once again return and along with them the buffalo. And perhaps even the grizzlies will once again return to the Hills to haunt those who, according to Isaac Cowie, killed 750 of them during one season in the days of Whoop-Up Country. They can return and join the deer, elk, antelope, and foxes that are still there.

CHAPTER 1

THE LAND AND ITS PEOPLE

THE LAND

The Cypress Hills are a flat-topped plateau covering an area of about 2,600 square kilometers (1,000 mi²) in southwestern Saskatchewan and southeastern Alberta. Glaciation bulldozed the surrounding terrain, with the ice mass splitting around the Hills and leaving them intact. They are a small remnant of a large plateau that existed in the region forty million years ago, but that was later almost totally eroded away. This finger of land, exposed above the glacier ice, may have been exploited by Pleistocene hunters as early as fifteen thousand years ago.

In more recent times, Native groups occupied the Hills seasonally as part of an annual movement to their hunting grounds out on the open plains in summer and to the shelter of hill country in winter. The Cypress Hills also contained an important resource for the Aboriginal peoples: the lodgepole pine. When the glaciers retreated from the plains, these trees survived as a key feature of this ecosystem, which is unique to the prairies. The only other environment where such pines could be found was in the Rocky Mountains. The Aboriginal peoples of the plains fashioned the poles for their lodges from the trees and used the smaller ones as the framework for dog and horse travois.

The Cypress Hills lie at the northern extension of an escarpment known as the Missouri Coteau. This escarpment stretches from the Souris River in the southeast, across the province of Saskatchewan and into Alberta. North and east of the escarpment lie the prairies—a rich grassland plain situated on a lowland glacial lake basin. To the northwest lie the Great Sand Hills of Saskatchewan, a vast desert area, the remains of a glacial lake. To the south of the Cypress Hills, the terrain is gently rolling to strongly rolling hills. This topography was created by the ground moraine left by glaciation some twenty thousand years ago.

The climate of the Cypress Hills area is one of dramatic extremes, fluctuating greatly from summer to winter. Summer temperatures may rise as high as thirty-eight degrees Celsius (100°F) with winter as low as minus forty-five degrees Celsius (–50°F). The precipitation in the area is generally low. The average rainfall is about thirty-six centimeters (14 in) and most of this rain generally falls in June. Often heavy rains cause rain-washing of the slopes in the coteau areas. The prevailing winds are from the west: warm, dry chinook winds often come from the west and southwest, while colder winter winds come from the northwest.

The vegetation of southwestern Saskatchewan is grassland; some undisturbed grassland habitat can still be found at Grasslands National Park just to the east of the Cypress Hills. Wild rose bushes and chokecherries grow on the hill slopes and can appear as thick growth along valley or coulee bottoms. To the northeast of the Missouri Coteau escarpment, the land is covered by mixed-grass prairies dotted with poplar. To the southwest are the short-grass plains that typically are characterized by the growth of sagebrush, with tree growth restricted to coulees and creek beds. According to geographers, the vegetation and climate have remained relatively unchanged over the past two thousand years.

The diverse habitat of the Cypress Hills has been able to support a large number of animals and birds. Before people arrived in large numbers during the last century, when the buffalo were still plentiful on the prairies, predators such as grizzly bears, mountain lions, and wolves could be found in the Hills. Today mostly smaller animals such as the lynx, bobcat, coyote, and fox remain, although frequently big game such as elk, moose, mule deer, and white-tailed deer can be spotted. The pronghorn antelope can also still be seen in the area, especially in the grassy meadows found in the gaps between the Hills. A variety of squirrels, the striped skunk, and badger inhabit this environment as well. The aspen woodlands provide refuge for the porcupine, raccoon, and chipmunk. Along the coulees of the Hills one is most likely to find Nuttal's cottontail and the snowshoe hare. Muskrat, mink, beaver, and a variety of weasels reside along the creeks and lakes of the Cypress Hills.

A great variety of birds can be found in the Hills—up to 207 species have been spotted. Of particular interest are the Audubon Warbler, Oregon Junco, and McGillivary's Warbler. The Hills are the breeding grounds for the Yellow-shafted Flicker and the Western Red-shafted Flicker. The larger trumpeter swans, cormorants, and Canada geese also breed in the Hills. Woodpeckers, ducks, robins, owls, buntings, swallows, bluebirds, loons, herons, hawks, eagles, and gulls are among some of the species that can still be found here.

The People

Scholars suggest that the first people crossed into North America over a land bridge into unglaciated regions of Alaska and the Yukon approximately 100,000 to 10,000 B.C. These big-game hunters from Asia pursued their game using stone-tool technology consisting of bifacial flaked knives and spear tips, as well as some microblades (thin, razor-sharp flakes of stone). As environmental conditions in the North deteriorated, these hunters migrated from the Alaska/Yukon region farther south through a corridor between two large ice sheets—the receding Laurentide to the east and the Cordilleran to the west. They moved down through this passageway into the center of the New World. By this time a new technology was evident, described by archaeologists as Fluted Point culture because of the style of arrowheads they used for hunting. The earliest use of the Cypress Hills environment might well have been in this era between 10,000 and 8,000 B.C.

The Fluted Point people survived by hunting big game such as mammoth, mastodon, and bison, as well as smaller animals such as camel, horse, sloth, caribou, and beaver. Evidence of the presence of these prehistoric mammals has been uncovered at the east end of the Hills around the present-day community of Eastend, Saskatchewan. Fluted Point people's clothing was made of hide and fur; their tools were made of bone and stone. Evidence of these early peoples has been found across southern parts of Canada, throughout the United States, and also in South America. Sites in northwestern Canada are limited.

The Fluted Point people were followed by the Plano people (8,000–4,000 B.C.), who were also big-game hunters. The Plano people expanded and refined earlier stone technology: new, distinctive flaking styles emerged, as did a greater variety of hunting tools. New tools such as stone hammers are found at Plano sites, as well as the earliest evidence of cremation burials. Sites of Plano peoples are found throughout the plains area. In the northern plains area they are thought to have hunted caribou, lived in family-sized tents, and to have created a stone technology unique to the plains. As the ice retreated, the Plano peoples moved eastward to the shores of the receding waters. Evidence of their habitation in Canada has been found as far east as the St. Lawrence River and in the Maritimes.

Approximately 6,000 B.C. the Early Plains people migrated northward from what is now the southern United States into Canada and onto the plains, bringing with them a new variety of notched projectile points and new hunting techniques. Coincident with the arrival of these new peoples was the arrival of a new dry climate (6,000–2,000 B.C.). The landscape was so hot that much of the archaeological record was obliterated, making identification of materials other than stone very problematic.

Following the Early Plains people were the Middle Plains people (4,000 B.C. to A.D. 500), a predominantly bison culture. Bison herds were the staple that provided raw material for food, shelter, and clothing. A complex social organization emerged from a people that needed to operate in large numbers in order to hunt successfully and process the buffalo. Bison herds were stampeded over cliffs or driven into pounds, ravines, or swales to be slaughtered, and the carcasses were processed into the products required by the people. Some of the many teepee rings throughout the Cypress Hills are from this early era. There is evidence that these bison hunters lived in tents that required stone weights to secure their sides at the circumference. These stones when rolled away were lasting markers of their presence. The remains of deformed dog hipbones are indications that the Middle Plains people used travois pulled by dogs. Evidence of burial sites with artifacts such as stone tools, eagle talons, copper from Lake Superior, and shell beads from Atlantic areas provide clues not only to their makers' belief systems but to their trade systems as well.

Pottery finds indicate a close trading relationship between plains people and those just south of them. Also, contact with forest people to the east and northeast is evident through the gradual emergence on the plains of the Siouan-speaking Assiniboin to the east and Algonquian speakers to the northwest. From the north came the Athapaskan-speaking Beaver, Sekani, and Sarsi (Tsuu T'ina) people, the latter eventually settling in southern Alberta. From the west and south came the Algonquian-speaking Blackfoot (Siksika) and Gros Ventre (Atsina) peoples; while from the southwest came the Kootenai-speaking peoples. Members of the Blackfoot Confederacy included the Siksika, the Peigans, and the Blood (Kainah).

There can be little doubt as to the presence of early humans in the Cypress Hills area. Remains of a campsite dating back some six thousand years have been discovered near Elkwater Lake on the Alberta side of the Cypress Hills, putting human presence in the Hills as early as the Fluted Point era. Also, within Fort Walsh National Historic Site, another site was found during installation of the fort's palisade. This site has been dated to periods from 1,200 B.C. to as early as 2,160 B.C., placing it in the Middle Plains period.

The era from A.D. 500 to approximately 1700, or direct European contact, was characterized by the culture of the buffalo-hunting peoples who then occupied the prairies. They were influenced by the Spanish far to the south, whose horses were traded onto the plains by the seventeenth century. There was also significant influence felt from the Missouri Valley, and for a period of time an agricultural settlement was established in southern Alberta that was an offshoot of the southern Missouri culture. Also, slowly moving to the north from Mexico and Central America through various trade networks were corn, squash, beans, sunflowers, and tobacco, and these plants began to be cultivated in parts of the southern plains.

The prairies were peopled by a variety of Indian tribes by 1700. The Prairie or Plains Cree occupied the eastern and central areas. The Dakota and Assiniboin (Stoney) were to the south of the Cree, while the Gros Ventre and the Blackfoot lived on the western extremity. The Plains Ojibwa or Saulteaux (Annishnawbe) lived to the east, with the Crow to the south of the Assiniboin.

The Cree, who dominated the central plains by the nineteenth century, were originally located in woodland areas to the west and north of the Great Lakes. They were a band society in which the ultimate unit of organization was the family. In small groups, they moved over their territory in search of game or to collect other food. Each family unit had an appointed leader. A number of bands could come together at various seasons, but this was rare and such groupings lasted for only short periods of time. There was no single chief for these bands and consequently there was little sense of unity among them. They had no controlling governing authority, but they did share a common language and had similar customs, and their social behavior and laws were determined by public opinion. The scarcity of fish and game in woodland areas made larger gatherings impossible. Unable to come together in great numbers, they rarely went to war with neighboring tribes; scattered in small groups in the woods, they were a difficult target for an enemy to attack.

In contrast with the family-centered Cree, traditional plains tribal society, such as that of the Blackfoot, had much larger units that stayed together for longer periods of time. On the open plains it was difficult to hide from neighboring tribes, making tribal cohesiveness a necessity for self-defense and creating more opportunities for military conflict than in the heavily treed woodlands. Food was also more abundant on the plains. Up to the mid-1870s, large herds of buffalo still migrated into Canadian territory, providing many plains peoples with a steady food supply and thus facilitating larger groups.

Greater organization and social control were demanded by the nature of life on the plains. The horse, especially, contributed to the development of a more organized political structure as it led to a highly mobile society. This was in contrast to the isolated woodland bands, who still moved on foot. The buffalo hunt required many horsemen, who needed to be tightly coordinated in the annual pursuit. These factors made it necessary to have a firmer political organization. In the spring, when all the people gathered together before the buffalo hunt, a council of men elected a chief. As a result, the plains people could be readily mobilized for both political and military purposes.

In the years after European contact, basic Indian social structures and belief systems did not undergo as dramatic a change as did their economic base. After more than two centuries of contact with European culture, the Indian way of life still stood in stark contrast to Euro-American culture. The plains tribes adapted to the economic changes they first faced with the arrival of the horse, then the gun, then the traders. But at its core, Aboriginal culture absorbed change on its own terms and retained beliefs and practices that enabled it to thrive on the plains.

Until the disappearance of the buffalo strained the relationship, the Métis were one group that was on reasonably good terms with the plains tribes, with whom they often intermarried. Métis and Canadien free traders are known to have used the Cypress Hills regularly from the start of the nineteenth century. Indeed, the Cypress Hills is an incorrect translation of the French *montagne aux cyprès. Cyprès* means cypress in standard French, but for French-Canadians and Métis it was the word used first for the jack pine and then for the lodgepole pine. A number of early sites are known to have been occupied by Métis families, and it has been estimated that there were approximately fifteen major Métis settlements and camp-sites throughout the Cypress Hills.

A number of Métis established themselves along the Whitemud River— some of whom are thought to have been émigrés from Red River before 1869. As well, some of the Métis leaving Red River after 1870 settled in the Cypress Hills area. Among this group was Riel's adjutant general, Ambroise Lepine, who settled near Elkwater Lake in a place called Ambroise Flats. Four major Métis camps are known to have existed by the late 1870s: one at East End (the present-day community of Eastend), one along Battle Creek near the future site of Fort Walsh, and two more at Head of the Mountain. There were also a number of smaller camps located in numerous coulees throughout the Cypress Hills.

The colonization of the Cypress Hills by Euro-Canadians has taken place in the much more recent past. In the mid- to late nineteenth century there were only a few White traders who worked along with the Métis as fur traders and suppliers of pemmican to what was left of the declining fur trade. In the 1870s the North-West Mounted Police arrived in the Cypress Hills to attempt to secure the Canadian half of the plains for settlement by Europeans. The police were followed by the ranchers, who began to raise cattle on the rangeland in and around the Hills. It is the story of those who traditionally used the Hills and those others who later came to the area to trade and settle that is the primary focus of this book.

2

THE BUFFALO AND THE FUR TRADE

BUFFALO

Life on the plains between A.D. 500 and 1700 revolved around the bison herds. The tribes around the Cypress Hills area depended on them for their survival and developed complex methods of hunting the huge herds that roamed across the southern plains. The two most basic forms of bison hunting were either the jump or the pound, though of course there were many varieties of them both. Archaeological evidence indicates that ancient hunters in the area around the Cypress Hills preferred driving bison into natural or constructed pounds rather than using jumps, because it was difficult to find terrain that lent itself to a jump site. Pounds were most likely to be found in wooded areas where the necessary brush to construct drive lanes could be found, as well as the timber necessary to construct corrals. This was in contrast with the buffalo jumps, which required rim-rock over which bison could be driven. Jump sites tend to be located closer to the Rocky Mountains.

The Gull Lake pound site on the northern fringes of the Cypress Hills has turned up some remarkable evidence. Here artifacts of three distinctive groups have been uncovered for the pre-contact period of the northern plains. Fluted points of the Plains and later Avonlea and Prairie peoples indicate their presence in the area as buffalo hunters. Algonquian-speaking Besant—a Middle Woodland (Avonlea Points) people—seem to have merged with Athapaskan invaders around A.D. 100, dominating the area until approximately A.D. 700. Much of the buffalo killing at this time was done with the bow and arrow that the Athapaskans brought from eastern Canada. Makers of Prairie points, likely Algonquian speakers, began to displace the established groups hunting with the older Avonlea points. Eventually the Prairie side-notched points emerged as the dominant buffalo-hunting technology. By A.D. 1300, the Plains side-notched variant of the Mississippian culture to the south appeared and seemed to dominate until the contact period with Europeans around 1700.

The bison-hunting culture of around 1700 encompassed four tribes that occupied the southern Canadian plains. These large tribal units would have hunted the bison with traditional bow-and-arrow methods, as well as with the gun traded down through Hudson Bay onto the plains from the seventeenth century on. The four major tribes were the Gros Ventre, the Assiniboin, the Blackfoot, and the Plains Cree.

The Blackfoot Confederacy traditionally occupied southern Alberta, though in the eighteenth century they moved up into Saskatchewan as far as the Eagle Hills, controlling an area between the North and South Saskatchewan rivers. At the height of their military power they occupied areas of southern Saskatchewan and north to the Battle River. The Gros Ventre occupied an area to the south and east of the Blackfoot and likely occupied southern Saskatchewan for lengthier periods of time than the Blackfoot. The Assiniboin, traditionally an extension of the Dakota people, inhabited an area east of the Gros Ventre and south of the Plains Cree, predominantly the area of northern Minnesota and southern Manitoba, but at the height of their power they extended as far north as Fort Carlton and as far west as the Cypress Hills. The Plains Cree were one of the most dominant groups on the prairies, occupying southern Manitoba, Saskatchewan, and extending into southern Alberta at the height of their influence in the nineteenth century. All four of these tribes would have occupied territory in and around the Cypress Hills.

Even though Europeans had crossed the Canadian plains since the late seventeenth century, the first observation of a buffalo pound was in 1772 by Mathew Cocking, a trader for the Hudson's Bay Company (HBC). The first observation of an actual hunt in progress was made by Alexander Henry the Elder, who was traveling with the Assiniboin in central Saskatchewan:

> About forty men and a great number of women . . . proceeded to a small island on the plain . . . women pitched a few tents . . . the chief led his hunters to its southern end where there was a powder enclosure. The fence was about four feet high, and formed of strong stakes of birch-wood, raffled with smaller branches of the same.[1]

Henry recalled robed runners leaving at daylight to entice the herd toward the pound. Bellows imitating the bison lured curious animals toward the decoyers until they were a short distance from the pound. When the animals were between the wings of the chute, the runners disappeared into movable portions of the chute walls and the buffalo gradually moved toward the pound entrance as the chute narrowed toward the corral. If bison veered from the course, people along the walls shook buffalo robes to put them back in the main stream of the herd. Once the buffalo were inside the pound, a string was pulled, sending a curtain made of buffalo robes over the entrance to prevent escape. Henry remembered seventy-two bison killed on the hunt he observed.

Into the nineteenth century plains people such as the Cree, Saulteaux, and Assiniboin were still using the buffalo as their economic mainstay, and many tribes were increasingly selling pemmican to fur-trade company posts. As the buffalo moved less frequently onto the northern plains, the HBC became more dependent on tribes to the south of them, in the vicinity of the Cypress Hills, to supply them with buffalo meat. In return for pemmican, the Company traded guns, knives, metal, cloth, pots, beads, liquor, and tobacco.

With the increased need for pemmican, the number of hunts undertaken by the Indians increased, but not the number of buffalo killed at a given hunt, which remained at about fifty to seventy animals. The most common time for a buffalo hunt was in late summer, fall, or early winter, when the animals had been fattened from their summer grazing. On some occasions there would be a number of drives in a season if the bison were located close to favored pound sites. In the early summer months, stationary herds of buffalo were sometimes hunted by encirclement, requiring a large number of people. This method was used to kill only a few buffalo. Bulls were not considered desirable for eating at this time, and only cows and calves were slaughtered. In late summer, the hunting of the buffalo was done on a grand scale. It required the participation of many people in a highly organized system as the hunt was intended to kill large numbers of buffalo.

The early-season hunt was one reason why individual bands came together in the spring. By then, fresh meat was required for food, sinews and bones of the buffalo were needed for new weapons, hides were wanted for clothing and to repair tents, and for trade. Small wintering parties of Indians would gather in larger tribal units as various bands emerged from valleys or hills in what is now eastern Saskatchewan and western Manitoba. In open areas they celebrated survival from winter and participated in the annual thirst or sun dance ceremony. In the ceremony, the Indians asked for the sun to give them strength for the buffalo hunt and bravery in war. It also served as a rite of passage for the younger members of the band. Throughout the late spring and summer the Indians spent time on the open prairie replenishing their food supplies, repairing their tents with buffalo skins, and gathering materials for weapons and food preparation.

The organization required for a hunt was complex and a division of labor was required for its successful execution. Special participants included the decoy runner, the poundmaker, and, for the Blackfoot, the holy women.

Considerable spiritual ritual accompanied the hunt. The poundmaker (for the Blackfoot, the holy women) was the initiator of the hunt. When no center tree was available, the poundmaker planted the medicine pole in the corral of the pound. Ceremonies were performed at the medicine pole and at the entrance of the pound to discover the favorable moment for the chase. The poundmaker then attached charms to the pole—usually a piece of red flannel two to three meters (2–3 yds) long, as well as tobacco and a bison's horn—and placed ceremonial objects at the entrance to the pound. Early in the mornings preceding a hunt the poundmaker beat a drum and recited hymns to conjure the spirits and appease the manitous (spirits) that guided the movements of the bison. The poundmaker would often remain at the medicine pole while the hunt was in progress. In the case of White Raven, an Assiniboin poundmaker, he hung suspended from the medicine pole for the duration of the hunt.

The buffalo hunt started when the herd was located. The process of guiding the buffalo into a funnel began many kilometers (miles) away from the actual killing ground. Stone cairns joined by people waving robes were arranged in two columns to form a corridor down which the buffalo were herded. Wide at the opening, the two lines narrowed as the buffalo were chased to their final destination: into a pound or over a buffalo jump. Another group of hunters was responsible for directing the buffalo toward the opening of the funnel and ensuring that the buffalo stayed on the course to the killing area. Whole buffalo bones lying on charcoal remains, as well as butchered bone scraps, are a common pattern to the finds at the Gull Lake pound site in the Cypress Hills, suggesting the process of burning the remains of a previous hunt prior to renewed butchering activity. After a successful hunt, there followed feasting. Failure to complete a hunt once begun had serious consequences as precious energy would have been wasted and locating a new herd meant the loss of valuable time, especially during times of want.

After a successful hunt, weeks were spent slaughtering the buffalo, then drying some of the meat. The women made the pemmican that helped carry the tribes through the winter months. Skins and furs were also prepared by the women through the late summer and fall for winter trade. In good years, some of the pemmican was traded to fur-trading companies, as were sinews, horns, and bones. Other parts of the buffalo were fashioned into tools and implements. Some of the hides were left whole. These were known as the "head and trail" robes and were more valuable than the "split robes" that were cut down the middle and then sewn together with sinew. These hides were packed together and transported by travois until the fall, when the people moved into the hilly areas.

When the buffalo were numerous the hunts meant abundant food, but life was obviously more desperate when the herds could not be found, as was the case toward the end of the nineteenth century. When this occurred the Indians were unable to gather enough food to survive over the winter months and they were often forced to camp by prairie lakes and live on fish they were able to catch there. This was increasingly the case for many Cree and Assiniboin in the late 1870s and early 1880s. As the buffalo became scarce in Canadian territory, plains people hunted this game in smaller groups, even individually. More and more Natives who now possessed both the gun and horse found hunting in groups less necessary.

Spring and early summer were a traditional time of war among various tribes as they competed with each other for buffalo-hunting territory. In the 1870s and 1880s, the buffalo remained in large numbers in what was primarily the Blackfoot territory of southern Alberta and northern Montana. The competition for the disappearing buffalo meant that there were frequent wars between groups that sought the same herds. As the buffalo declined in number, conflicts increased as more people competed for fewer animals.

As fall arrived and the first snow of winter fell, the large tribal groupings that had moved across the plains together through the summer months would break up into smaller bands or family units and then proceed into the wintering hills. For hundreds, perhaps even thousands of years, plains tribes had wintered in forest havens such as the Cypress Hills. In the shelter of the hilly regions, among poplar and birch copses, the people were able to find fuel and could more easily pursue small game. This game would supplement the pemmican gathered in summer. Indeed stray herds of buffalo were often found in sheltered valleys during the winter season. The tribes lived close to the rich resources offered by the natural world around them. They traditionally carried few material goods because these were not necessary when the surrounding land and animals provided such an easily accessible bounty.

As traders increasingly came to the area, winter was the time when the Indians and Métis came to the trading posts to exchange their buffalo robes and furs for the goods and foodstuffs offered by the traders. During the summer there was little demand for European goods. The traders arrived in the Cypress Hills in late summer or early fall with their bull-trains loaded with trade goods. If the previous year's fort was still standing, the traders occupied the same site. If not they would choose a new spot to build on, one that might place them in a more favorable position than their competitors.

As winter arrived the traders busied themselves with the business of trade, and the plains tribes and Métis began arriving with their summer's catch.

The Indians and Métis traded for pots, kettles, traps and other metal goods, large quantities of patterned flannel to make clothes, as well such amenities as liquor and tobacco. Many also purchased beads for their artwork and items like mirrors simply for amusement. This trade would continue throughout the late fall and winter as the Indians looked for the best bargains they could get from the competing traders. As the winter wore on, the Indians hunted individually, pursuing buffalo and other smaller game. The hides of these animals would then be taken to the traders.

Trapping for furs was now a major activity and likewise the furs would be brought into the posts. As they depleted their own food resources, the Indians increasingly traded at the posts for food. Bacon, flour, tea, and other staples were in great demand at these times. In the most desperate years the tribes camped close to the forts as they became more and more dependent on food from the traders. The hungrier and weaker the Indians became, the less they were able to hunt and trap.

By the late 1870s, the end of trading season and the arrival of spring no longer meant hunting for the buffalo as it once did. This former cycle of life was over forever and a new way of life awaited the Indians with the treaties and life on the reserves.

THE FUR TRADE

The nineteenth century was a major watershed for Plains Indians. Ahead of them lay adaptation to Anglo-Canadian culture and subsistence agriculture and a life that was controlled by government regulations. Behind them lay a long tradition of adaptation to the forest and plains environments.

The Cree, who became a dominant group as a result of the fur trade, were primarily woodland people in the early seventeenth century. They occupied an area between Hudson Bay and Lake Superior, and some of the westernmost Cree occupied territories into present-day Manitoba. They were basically a hunter-gatherer band society. They used canoes, collected wild rice, and were enemies of the Dakota to the south.

Through the explorations of Anthony Henday in the mid-eighteenth century, the HBC learned that Cree to the south and west of Hudson Bay were acting as the primary middlemen in the fur trade. As they moved out of the forests south of the Bay, the Cree controlled the prairie river systems and blocked the eastward access from the plains to Hudson Bay. Not only did Henday find the Cree trading with the French, and later with the independent traders, but they were collecting prime furs at the expense of the English.

By the 1770s the consequences of this competition became clear. "The Indians traded their best beaver and marten inland (to the French and free traders), then came down to the company posts hoping to exchange the remnants of their catch for the Brazil tobacco and Beaver goods which the Canadians could not supply."[2]

As shrewd businessmen, the Cree were playing one buyer against the other, extracting the best prices they could for their furs. By 1773 the HBC decided to move into the interior to combat the increasing trade in furs taken by the free traders based on the St. Lawrence River. The Company moved westward in 1774, establishing a post at Cumberland House, a site between the Bay and the Saskatchewan river system and along the Athabaska river system. By the 1780s the HBC had also established posts southwards at Rainy River, Red Lake, and Lake of the Woods to make inroads into the area now dominated by its competitors. By the turn of the century the Company was at the last barrier before the Pacific Ocean— the Rocky Mountains.

It was this move inland that weakened the stranglehold the Cree held on the fur trade that had been, until then, centered on the Bay. As the HBC moved farther inland, they were able to trade directly with the Blackfoot, Peigan, and the Blood, among others. Competition between the North West Company (NWC), headquartered in Montreal, and the HBC escalated through these years and resulted in a desperate drive to gain dominance of the trade. This had dramatic consequences for the traditional trading role enjoyed by the Cree. "As the Canadian and Hudson's Bay men moved onto the Saskatchewan, so the Western Cree and Assiniboin lost their function as middlemen in the trade, and drifted onto the plains beyond the North Saskatchewan, where they kept their links with the companies, but rather as buffalo hunters and provisioners."[3] With this displacement the Cree again had to adjust to changing economic realities.

By 1821 the heated rivalry between the NWC and HBC was threatening the existence of the latter. The result was a merger of the two companies, followed by an era characterized by the sound administration of the new HBC business by the energetic and efficient Sir George Simpson. Two decades later, with demand for beaver in decline, the Company's fortunes fell. The halcyon days were gone and the Indians who had long been linked to the economic system introduced by the Europeans were not only geographically displaced but were now economically displaced as well. A certain dependence on European goods had grown among the Cree, but while the profitability of the trade had now lessened, the demand for these goods had not. Thus they began to look elsewhere for a livelihood.

By the time of Confederation, a national policy was in place to bring prosperity to Canada and to the West by protective tariffs, railway development, and ambitious schemes to bring settlers to the prairies. With the HBC in decline, the Indians and Métis were no longer able to profit from the fur trade and the buffalo had disappeared, the last big hunt occurring in the late 1870s. The future for Aboriginal peoples depended increasingly on economic opportunities and accommodations offered by the Canadian expansion into the West. The 1870s and 1880s were a transitory period for the Plains Cree as they began to rely on treaties, reserves, and federal government policies that promised them a new livelihood.

The role of the Cree in the fur trade, their subsequent move onto the plains after the buffalo, and the resulting diplomatic systems that emerged have only recently been explored by scholars. It is perhaps a telling comment on the bias of early Western Canadian historians that comparatively little was written about the role played by the Indians in the history of the fur trade.

Three distinct phases can be identified between the first direct contact with Europeans and the end of the fur-trade era around 1870. The first period began in 1670 with the alliance between the Cree and Blackfoot situated to the west. The second phase was the period when the Cree developed a stronger alliance with the Mandan to the south, who supplied them with horses. Historian John Milloy labels this phase as the "Horse Wars" era dating from 1810–50, a time when the Cree were increasingly acquiring horses and were seeking alliances to the west.

During the early nineteenth century the Cree were able to exist in their centralized tribal way of life because they maintained many of their traditional social and cultural values. Status was still gained by common activities within the tribe and not by individual conquest or accumulation of wealth. They kept the tradition of distribution through gift giving and a "disdain for material possessions."[4] This was in contrast to the Blackfoot, who were growing more toward a social system based upon status through accumulation of wealth and a decentralized structure of power. The gun and horse were absorbed into Cree society without drastic changes to their social structure, although some adjustment had to take place. Tribalism remained the strongest bond for the Cree during the years up to 1850. At the end of this period they were the most dominant tribe on the plains. The once-powerful Blackfoot, enemies not only of the Kootenai, Shoshoni, and Crow, but now also the Cree, had begun to seek peace with the Cree.

The third phase is labeled the "Buffalo Wars" period of 1850–70. During these wars, the Assiniboin and Cree came together as allies against the

Blackfoot Confederacy. These wars were critical to the Cree and Assiniboin as fewer and fewer buffalo were coming into their territory. The years of the Buffalo Wars were characterized by dwindling buffalo herds. The Cree blamed the Métis and Whites for the decline but did not openly clash with them since they still relied on their trade goods. The Cree partnership with the Whites was no longer as useful to them as it had once been. The Cree had never been manipulated by Whites, but made their own choices based on what was in their best self-interest. Buffalo was most important to them in the mid-1800s; however, they, along with their allies the Assiniboin, were unable to drive the Blackfoot out from prime buffalo territory, and by the late 1870s the great herds were gone.

INDIAN WOMEN IN THE BUFFALO AND FUR-TRADE ERA

Male observers in the early contact period tended to ignore or downplay or misunderstood the role and status of women in Indian society. The observers generally fell back on images they had from their own society of women as lower-class people, and they presented Indian women as slaves, drudges, and beasts of burden, indicating that they were total subordinates and under the control of men. As well they reinforced images of women as being of questionable moral standard, emphasizing that Indian marriages required no legal or religious status, that divorce was readily accepted, and that people were allowed free sexual expression from a very early age. All this was evidence of weak moral standards in the eyes of Europeans.

There have been some efforts to discuss gender relations and gender differences in Indian cultures and the extent to which these were reshaped by post-colonial forces. Gender as a social construct reflects and defines the social identities of women and men. Ideas of gender provide culturally determined roles that become models for behavior. Concepts of gender are ideological, and they explain and reinforce cultural evaluations of appropriate male and female activity and identity. Assignment of roles in society can be an indication of the gender relations in that society.

One school of thought emphasizes the egalitarian nature of pre-contact society, that Indian women were an esteemed and essential part of their societies until the imposition of Judeo-Christian beliefs. Anthropologist Eleanor Leacock, working among the Montagnais-Naskapi of Quebec, argues that in this hunter-gatherer society there was equality; that the women made essential economic contributions; that they had an important voice in the decision-making process of the band; that they had autonomy and power in domestic and reproductive concerns; that while they had separate spheres of activity this did not imply inequality for women; that the fact that tasks were split along gender lines did not mean that women were helpless without men, or vice versa. Men and women were mutually dependent; they controlled the terms and arrangements of their own work.[5]

The fur trade changed all this. It introduced a system of political, economic, and social organization that was incompatible with traditional Indian culture. The newcomers intended to accumulate capital, the commodity they were after was fur, and they required a source of labor to produce that commodity. In order to use Indians as a source of labor they had to dominate and reorganize Indian society. The relationship of equality between the sexes had to end, and relations of exploitation had to replace the former relations of cooperation. This transformation took place over an extended period of time.

Those that emphasize gender inequality in Indian societies before the arrival of the Europeans often suggest that European contact meant liberation to Indian women; that as their lot was improved, their prospects brightened. Many within this school of thought emphasize that women were not pawns of Europeans; that they were not used against their will; that they were "active agents" and not "passive victims." Women, it is maintained, were shrewd and pragmatic and they adapted to the pressures of colonization. The image of women as passive victims, these scholars argue, as pawns in the colonial situation, is in need of revision. Increasingly scholars are arguing that Native women had choices and exercised them.

In a gender study of nineteenth-century plains society among the Teton Dakota, Assiniboin, Blackfoot, and Gros Ventre, Alan Klein examines the effects of the hide trade and the horse among these peoples.[6] Klein argues that these trades had far-reaching implications for the status of women. The traditional patterns of life still evident among plains peoples in the eighteenth century were remarkably altered by the nineteenth.

Klein shows eighteenth-century plains life as one that was characterized by foot travel. Collective hunting methods dominated, while individual methods were secondary. Women made vital contributions through their gathering, since the hunt was often precarious. At times bands had to survive upon the efforts of women. Klein describes these societies as egalitarian because of the nature of their hunting, which was collective. Women were required as part of the collective hunt, so their position was roughly comparable to that of men. There were also few inequities of wealth as people produced mainly for their own use and consumption.

Changes arrived with the introduction of the horse. The horse was introduced as a privately held commodity controlled by men. Klein argues that hunting became individualized, only using large groups of hunters at certain times, as increased mobility meant that collective efforts were no longer as essential. Individual ownership of the kill was also introduced (previously the kill had been collectively owned) and the choice cuts belonged to the man who killed the animal. Women were now absent from the hunt, which had become the domain of men.

The buffalo-hide trade, introduced about 1820, introduced a new trade in European goods. This brought new technology and a new prosperity to the Indians—and a greater demand for hides. There was also a change in labor patterns as the division of labor between the sexes became more strictly defined. To meet increased demand, there was increased specialization of labor: men became the producers of raw materials and women became the processors of these.

The rise in the hide trade dramatically increased the amount of time women spent tanning hides. It was estimated that it took one woman approximately ten days to tan a single buffalo robe, but that if she was freed from other tasks it could be accomplished in just three days. While men could provide women with raw materials with relative ease while the herds were abundant, women's work was far more time-consuming. The average man could supply at least two women with enough hides to tan. Klein sees the rise in the demand for tanners as a cause of increased polygamy. Other methods also appear to have been used to increase the labor supply, such as the capture of women from other tribes.

Ethnohistorian Richard Perry also observed that while women's labor was at a premium, their position was in jeopardy—they labored more and enjoyed the work less. The economy changed from one preoccupied with consumption to one that concentrated on production for exchange. There was increased prosperity, but only for men—those men who owned horses and could purchase trade goods. There was an erosion of women's position and status, while men were increasingly free to pursue wealth. Women lost the ability to control status-bearing goods. The result of all this was that in the nineteenth century men were favored over women and the individual was favored over the group. Even if women were making choices, they were still losing both political and economic status. As the material basis of plains culture altered, the egalitarian basis of plains culture was undermined by a new economic order.

CHAPTER 3

WHOOP-UP COUNTRY

The circumstances that brought people to the Canadian Northwest in the nineteenth century were rooted in the fur-trading activities of the first half of the century and were propelled by the rapid rise in the price of buffalo robes in the latter half. Alcohol had long been used in the fur trade, though in the 1860s and 1870s its use became even more widespread than previously. After 1821, the HBC was largely successful in curbing the trade in Rupert's Land, although some limited use of liquor continued.[1] Alcohol was a more important part of the operations of the American Fur Company (AFC), albeit curbed somewhat by an 1832 Act of Congress prohibiting the sale of spirits in Indian territory. In violation of the law, the AFC continued to smuggle and trade alcohol, and in the hard times after 1861, whiskey smuggling helped the company stay afloat.[2]

In the late 1860s, a number of factors converged which, for a brief few years, sent the bull-trains of "Indian traders" creaking north from Fort Benton, Montana, to exploit an area that had been largely neglected by the fur trade. For a short period, until it ended abruptly on the Canadian side with the arrival of the North-West Mounted Police in 1874–75, this region received an exciting, though sometimes bitter, taste of the American "Wild West." Whoop-Up Country was characterized by the whiskey trade. South of the border it is now northern Montana and north of the 49th parallel, southern Alberta and southwestern Saskatchewan. The expression "whoop it up" describes a run for the border by traders who sold whiskey to the Indians as they were trying to avoid being rounded up by either the army or the police. The names of Forts Whoop-Up, Slide-Out, Standoff, Robbers Roost, and Whiskey Gap illustrate the character and atmosphere of the times.

In 1862, with the discovery of gold in the mountains around Helena, what was soon to become Montana Territory boomed. When the gold rush subsided, many of the former prospectors, led by seasoned fur traders and joined by soldiers released from the Union and Confederate armies after the end of the American Civil War, remained in the area as free traders. In 1864 Montana Territory was created and U.S. marshals were attempting to enforce federal law. Border patrols were present, even if poorly staffed. As a result whiskey traders had to keep an eye out on the U.S. side of the border. To evade the "long arm of the law," the Fort Benton merchants logically looked to Canada, where, although the sale of liquor to Indians had been made illegal by an 1867 Act of Parliament, superseded by a North-West Territories Ordinance of 1870, there was absolutely no enforcement. The trading of whiskey could boost a trader's profits substantially. In 1854 a clear profit of 45 cents could be made on trading a $9.67 gun for $16.00 worth of buffalo robes.[3] Proof alcohol cost the trader $3.25 to $6.00 a gallon—diluted and spiced up it could bring up to $50.00 in hides. In one rate of exchange, two robes were traded for one large glass of "rot-gut" whiskey.[4]

On June 15, 1870, the Helena *Daily Herald* announced that Irish-born adventurer John Jerome Healy and his business partner, Alfred B. Hamilton, had netted the impressive sum of fifty thousand dollars trading in the British possessions to the north, and concluded that this was " not very bad" for a six months' cruise among the Indians across the border.[5] These two businessmen from Sun River, with an estimated two hundred liters (50 gal) of raw alcohol and backed by Hamilton's uncle I. G. Baker, had built Fort Whoop-Up in 1869 at the junction of the St. Mary's and Oldman rivers, the first important whiskey post on the Canadian side of the border.[6] Baker was a partner in the duo's Sun River post in Montana, from which the supplies to Whoop-Up were now channeled. In the next five years or so dozens of other traders based in Montana crossed the as-yet-unmarked international boundary and tried their luck at the risky, but extremely profitable business of trading point blankets, brass wire, smoking tobacco, and diluted whiskey to the Indians across the Canadian line.[7]

It was the price paid for buffalo robes that was the traders' major motive to come to Canada. The price of beaver declined in the 1840s and other furs became more prominent: muskrat, mink, deer, bear, raccoon, fox, skunk, and increasingly buffalo—at this time made primarily into throws for open sleighs and wagons.[8] In 1846 a buffalo robe brought a trader $3.00, a decade later $3.50, and by the early 1870s, $5.50 to $6.00, with a fine robe from Saskatchewan country paying up to $12.00.[9] In the late 1860s a Benton merchant could sell a number-one quality hide for $16.50 to a St. Louis wholesaler, who would then get up to $25.00 for it in the retail trade.[10] In 1871 demand for buffalo robes was further increased when a U.S. tannery developed a new treatment to change raw buffalo skins into leather tougher than cowhide, exactly what was needed for industrial belting in the industrializing eastern United States. The hides from the northern herds were the best, being thicker than those from animals found farther south.

In 1870 a total of 5,000 buffalo hides were shipped out of Canada; in 1872 the T. C. Power Co. alone sent 15,400 robes down the Missouri, many of these from Canada; and by 1876 some 75,000 were transported east from Fort Benton.[11] The robes were moved by steamboat to warehouses in St. Louis, a system that put the HBC at an extreme disadvantage as it was unable to move the large bulky cargoes of robes with such ease.[12]

Traders from Montana surged northward in their anxious pursuit of the quick money the buffalo-robe trade offered. The harvest of the buffalo was pursued with such vigor that gradually the exploitation of the herds led to their depletion. Mercantile companies, centered in Fort Benton, encouraged these developments and supplied credit to traders, allowing them to venture into Canadian territory and winter on the Canadian side of the border. There they traded with the Indian and Métis populations of these territories. The credit supplied to these trading partners was in the form of goods on consignment that were carried by bull-trains northward. Here the goods were exchanged with "Indian traders" for the desired furs and robes. Thus the substructure of this trade was established along a north-south axis as traders went into Canada each season. The Indian and Métis peoples occupying the territory moved in their own seasonal cycles, as the climate and terrain allowed, and in the Cypress Hills and southern Alberta they came into contact with the Benton traders.

The HBC also maintained a presence in the region. Although the HBC no longer sought furs in the southern districts, where furs were now scarce, and concentrated its efforts farther north where the fur trade was more profitable, the area south of the Red Deer River remained important to the Company because of the buffalo in the region. The pemmican made from these animals made the territory indispensable to the functioning of the HBC, and they traded for it with the Indian and Métis peoples. Pemmican was the simplest way of feeding men in the territory. Its preparation remained what it had been for plains people for centuries: dried buffalo meat was placed in large troughs with berries, such as saskatoons, then melted grease was added and the whole concoction mixed with a wooden shovel. This mixture of meat, berries, and grease was then packed in rawhide bags, which were sewn shut and shipped out for use. This hearty food kept for months, even years.

Following their traditional cycles of movement, Indians and Métis moved to the shelter of the Cypress Hills in winter. There they sought out the crude log shacks, sometimes graced with the name "fort," constructed by the American traders to bargain for goods the traders brought with them from Fort Benton. There were four main groups who traversed this territory. First were the plains tribes, which included the Cree, Assiniboin, Gros Ventre, Blackfoot, Dakota, Crow, Sarsi, and Blood. Second, there were the Métis, who were being displaced from their once-prominent role as tripmen and freighters for the once-powerful but now declining HBC. Third, there were the traders, like Moses Solomon and Abel Farwell who represented American commercial interests farther south. And last, there were groups of so-called "wolfers," who hunted wolves for their highly prized fur. There was usually an uneasy truce and respect, sometimes bred out of fear, that prevented violence from breaking out between these groups. But there were also lurking racial hatreds, especially between the wolfers and the Indians.

The Métis dispersed across the prairies in great numbers after the Red River Resistance of 1869–70. According to Isaac Cowie, an HBC trader in the area, many of these Métis were sympathetic to the Americans or had ties with Métis living in American territory. Thus they gravitated toward the traders at Benton and Helena. The consequences of this were obviously detrimental to the HBC:

> The American traders were not long in taking advantage of these circumstances, and in 1872 they established whiskey trading-posts at Cypré Hills and to the west, the steam boating facilities on the Missouri giving them great advantages over us; and their acquaintance among the Blackfoot.[13]

American Métis had long provided labor, guiding, and interpreting skills for American fur-trading companies operating in the Missouri River system. Often identified as "Canadian" or "French," many actually had their origins in the Métis settlements of the Great Lakes region.[14]

By the 1870s the Métis made up a large part of the population of the northern portion of Whoop-Up Country. Reasons for their migration west from Manitoba included discontent with the HBC fur-trade monopoly, political and social discontent in Red River, and increased demand for buffalo leather. Good prices for robes and economical goods could be found at Fort Benton because of the inland port's transportation advantage. In Canada, the diminishing buffalo herds were now concentrated in southern Alberta and the southwestern tip of Saskatchewan. All of these factors led to large Métis settlements in the Cypress Hills, and at Wood Mountain, Milk River, Frenchman (Whitemud) River, and Marias River. The trade in robes and pemmican could be lucrative—one large pemmican contract for the Fort Peck Indian Agency required the meat from two thousand slaughtered buffalo, but this bounty lasted only a few short years.

By the late 1870s the slaughter of buffalo and exploitation of game had exhausted the resources in the Cypress Hills area. The final destruction of the buffalo took but a few years: from the early 1860s to the early 1880s. The uncontrolled killing continued right to the end. By 1877 the only major herds left in Saskatchewan were concentrated south and west of the Cypress Hills along the Milk River. Famine accompanied the disappearing buffalo for the Métis and Indian peoples. In addition, a large fire in the Cypress Hills in 1879 made the presence of game, needed to support the wintering traders, scarce. By 1880 the Métis winterers of the Hills began to leave, many heading toward the Missouri River basin. Others moved to settlements along the Peace River in northern Alberta and in north and central Saskatchewan.[15] The last wild buffalo killed in the Cypress Hills was shot by Robert McCutcheon on Irvine Flats in 1882.

One group of Métis who used and settled in the Cypress Hills were those from the Wood Mountain area. The Métis who settled at Wood Mountain were one of two main groups who left Red River after 1869–70. The other larger group of Métis settled farther south and west along the Milk River, closer to the disappearing buffalo herds. Many Métis from Wood Mountain moved west with the diminishing buffalo, and in the winter of 1875–76 the Wood Mountain community was almost totally deserted as the Métis settled in the Cypress Hills.

The practice of leaving the main settlements during winter to pursue the buffalo was one that was well known and is described as follows by a missionary:

> Our Indians and Half-breeds call "hibernation" a place they have chosen to live in during winter, and prepare themselves for hunting expeditions. To that effect, they build in the prairies temporary dwellings which they abandon at the melting of snow, and in which, meanwhile, they will find a safe cover. Usually the place is chosen only after a serious inspection. Indeed, it is necessary to find fire-wood and timber in the vicinity and, moreover, to be near the buffalo herds which supply them with meat and hides.[16]

The Cypress Hills became the temporary home for a wide variety of people as the last straggling buffalo could still be found there in winter. In previous times only the most daring had entered into this territory without the advantage of numbers or superior weapons. The presence of both the Cree and Blackfoot was feared. But by the 1870s Reverend Clovis Rondeau observed many different people in the Hills. Of the year 1873 Rondeau wrote:

> The place is now the perpetual rendez-vous of all Indian tribes, not only of Canada, but also of the United States. Last winter, a tribe coming from the other side of the Missouri River had

almost 1500 lodges there. The Nez Perces had 6 lodges. There were from 200 to 300 lodges of heaper [sic], Crees, Assiniboin and others. There also were the remains of a numerous tribe which, after having plundered and killed everything in certain districts of Oregon and covered a distance of 1500 miles on its flight to Canada, met the American cavalry at the frontier before reaching Wood Mountain. Those unlucky people arrived in a deplorable condition, worn out with fatigue, no shoes, no cloths [sic], no food, almost all of them wounded.

Such is the population that the hope of good hunting had attracted to Cypress Hills last winter.

There are also 200 families of French Canadian Half-breeds. That place has therefore become, during winter, a considerable centre, full of activity. The buffaloes have attracted all these people, who are a mixture of all races and religions.[17]

By 1877 the majority of the Métis who had wintered in the Cypress Hills the previous three winters had moved back to Wood Mountain. Their priest, Father Jules De Corby, identified the major Métis settlements at the Cypress Hills, Wood Mountain, Milk River, Whitemud River, and Porcupine Creek. Each settlement was estimated to included fifty to eighty families. The constant movement of the Métis during these years was the cause of great concern for the priests and the Catholic establishment in general. The priests in the field reported that children knew only about hunting, furs, and hides. They saw the priests but once a year and this was not enough to learn their catechism. None of them attended school:

This life of hibernation is far from being favourable to the moral and material progress of those Christians who in their attachment to the religion, often forget its precepts. In the near future, they will be compelled, although they do not want to do that, to settle down and do some farming because the buffaloes will probably disappear forever on account of the destruction of which they are the object.[18]

It was unusual to witness much violence between traders and the Indians and Métis, even though over-consumption of alcohol and disappearing buffalo did lead to isolated clashes. The relationships between groups could be amicable, if cautious, even without a police force present. The one group disliked by both traders and Indians were the wolfers, whose poisoned bait, intended for wolves, killed many animals, including Indian dogs. Both Whites and Métis feared the chances of escalating violence during the stressful times as the buffalo declined.

The region around the Cypress Hills was left primarily to the Indians and the Métis *hivernants* (winterers). By the 1860s the latter worked as freighters on various routes through the Northwest, as tripmen on the water brigades, or as employees of the Canadian or American fur-trade companies; however, their primary job was as provisioners for the fur trade as they hunted the diminishing buffalo herds. It was as pemmican provisioners that the Métis occupied the Cypress Hills. They needed to kill large numbers of buffalo, prepare their product, and then transport the goods to trading posts throughout the Northwest. Much of it went directly north to Fort Pitt, which was a major pemmican distribution point for the rest of the Canadian Northwest.

For the plains tribes, the area around the Hills had become a buffer zone, largely due to the Buffalo Wars between the Cree and Blackfoot, and the Métis moved into the gap to exploit its rich resources and to use it as a base for the buffalo hunt. The pemmican manufactured during these years was transported in Red River carts or on barges north to the Athabasca and Mackenzie departments of the HBC and northeast up the Saskatchewan river system. When buffalo leather increased in demand, the Métis were in a strategic position to hunt the dwindling buffalo herds for the robes desired by merchants, both at Red River and at Fort Benton.

In 1869–70 Rupert's Land was formally transferred to the authority of the Canadian government, but this was initially little more than symbolic as there was no attempt to place a Canadian presence in the region. The HBC eventually did make some efforts to increase its fur-trading activities in southern Alberta and Saskatchewan. In the fall of 1871, clerk Isaac Cowie established a wintering post at the east end of the "Cypré Hills" at a spot called Chapel (later Chimney) Coulee. In 1873 another temporary HBC post was erected, farther north in the Sand Hills, near the Elbow of the South Saskatchewan River. The Cypress Hills were described by Cowie, at that time, as a neutral territory into which his Indian guides would not venture, but also an area rich in game particularly "red deer" (elk) and grizzly bears.

The site chosen by Cowie was ideal for winter trading as chinook winds frequently cleared the hills of snow and made access to the fort easier. During the early 1870s the area was in the shadow of the Blackfoot Confederacy, who did not physically occupy the Cypress Hills but frequently ventured into them. At this time Métis traders, most from Red River, were the most prominent group in the area and were established, according to Cowie, at Wood Mountain, Pinto Horse Butte, and the Eagle Hills. Cowie remembered that some Métis were involved in the whiskey trade, but suggests that HBC traders were not.

41

Cowie's trade was good. In the spring of 1872 Cowie and his Métis assistants were so laden down with furs and buffalo robes that they were forced to leave forty buffalo carcasses behind. Cowie relied heavily on the help of Métis Xavier Denomie who was able to guide, by day or night, in difficult weather. The trip to Qu'Appelle in that season was expected to take two weeks, but took twice as long because of the unpredictable spring and the difficulties the horses had breaking through layers of crusted snow, produced by alternating extremes of thawing then freezing. By the end of the season Cowie had obtained 750 grizzly bear skins and 1,500 "red deer" hides:

> Most of these were unprimed summer bearskins—mere hides which every hunter was using for cart covers instead of the ordinary buffalo bull hides, for large numbers had been slain off horseback in a run on the prairie. Many of them were of immense size approaching that of a polar bear; one skin measured by me was thirteen feet [4 m] from tip to tail. This material reservation of grizzly and elk soon ceased to them after the neutrality of the Hills had ceased owing to our invasion.[19]

The Cypress Hills were still a place of danger. Cowie indicates that many hunters and traders were shot carelessly by unskilled woodsmen who mistook their red buffalo-skin jackets for red deer. In addition, friction between various Indian groups led to conflict, and Cowie occasionally came across the remains of a camp that had been attacked. Such was the case in 1872 when he discovered a camp of careless Assiniboin who had been destroyed in a raid by a band of Blackfoot. It was probably because of this and the fear of American whiskey traders that Cowie did not return to the Hills in the fall of 1872.[20]

Except for these brief forays into southern Saskatchewan, the HBC was content to keep its trade with the Cree and Assiniboin centered at Qu'Appelle and Last Mountain House. Closer to Blackfoot territory the trade was still conducted from Rocky Mountain House, but in the 1871–72 season a mere 242 robes were taken in at the fort because the Blackfoot preferred to go south to the Americans. By 1874, the post was staffed with only two men, and it was finally abandoned the following year.

Before the influx of free traders in the late 1860s, Whoop-Up Country had been visited by several parties of gold prospectors seeking gold deposits like those found in Montana. These expeditions included those of 1862 and 1864, the former sponsored by the AFC, and in 1866–67 Canadians on the way to Montana gold fields crossed the area. The best known prospecting party was the McClelland expedition of 1868, which included

John Jerome Healy as guide. At least three other future whiskey traders gained an intimate knowledge of the area with these expeditions: Joe Kipp, son of James Kipp and Earth Woman; George Houk; and Dave Ackers, the latter being the last owner of infamous Fort Whoop-Up.[21]

The demise of the AFC in 1865 left the Missouri River basin trade open to new commercial concerns. The first of the firms that attempted to continue the trade included the small outfit of Durfee and Peck, and the Northwestern Fur Company (NWFC). However, these companies, based solely on fur trading, were unable to compete in the new environment of the 1860s and 1870s. In 1869 the NWFC abandoned the trade above Fort Buford and in 1870 it ceased operations entirely. New, more broadly based and therefore more stable, mercantile companies sprang up to fill the void.[22] Among these were Carroll and Steell; Murphy, Neel, and Co.; W. J. Wetzel; and J. D. Weatherwax; but most important were I. G. Baker and Bro. and T. C. Power and Bro., the new "merchant princes" of Benton.[23]

The inland port's strategic location and Baker and Power's monopoly of the steamboat lines were the ultimate keys to success for these companies.[24] Isaac Gilbert Baker, after trading to agency Indians, was appointed chief clerk at Fort Benton in 1864. The year after the AFC collapsed, he founded a general mercantile business with his brother George, becoming "the first merchandiser in the area."[25] Their new company began supplying goods to army posts and the ever-increasing numbers of settlers and miners.[26] They soon had a rival in the trade—the company of Thomas C. Power. Power, who came West as a government surveyor, arrived in Fort Benton in 1867 with his brother. They began selling a stock of goods brought from the East, to the same people as Baker.[27] These merchants drew on their business connections in the eastern U.S. to harness the pools of capital released after the American Civil War.[28] They began to supply small itinerant traders like Moses Solomon and Abel Farwell, who dealt directly with the Indians.

The "Indian trade" in Whoop-Up Country changed considerably after the 1850s. The Blackfoot came to terms with the U.S. government in 1855 with the Judith River Treaty, and any remaining aggressiveness in the tribe had been crushed by General Eugene Baker in January of 1870. In addition, Blackfoot desire for items of European manufacture had been steadily increasing since mid-century. The goods of the traders had been success-fully incorporated into Blackfoot culture.[29] These factors combined to break down the old Blackfoot resistance to trade.[30]

There were now two basic types of Indian traders in Montana. The first were the licensed and heavily bonded traders who traded legally with agency or treaty Indians, or set up at army posts. In the summer of 1868 the U.S. government drastically limited the number of licenses issued and so I. G. Baker, on the Marias River, and the NWFC, on the Teton, became the only fur companies in the area able to legitimately conduct trade with the Indians.[31] The second group were the unlicensed traders who could not legally trade with reservation Indians or in "Indian territory," although what exactly that was, at any given time, was often difficult to determine. They conducted their illicit dealings wherever they could establish a trading post and attract customers.[32] These traders obtained "outfits" on credit or in partnership from merchants or licensed traders, and repaid in furs and pelts. The illegal traders usually included alcohol, a substance prohibited in the Indian trade by U.S. law since 1832, in their stock of goods.[33] The free traders soon moved into the area north of the 49th parallel where there was a total lack of policing. They diverted furs away from Red River and the HBC, southward to the American companies in Fort Benton. The American traders were joined by Métis *hivernants* of such regions as the Cypress Hills, who took advantage of the higher prices offered by the American companies.

Baker and Power had founded their Fort Benton operations as the gold rush of the mid-1860s exhausted itself, and in a search for new profits these companies eagerly began to supply the illegal free traders. This trade, especially when it was extended into Canada, laid the foundations for the fortunes of the Benton merchants.[34] Power, in particular, prospered and expanded into the wholesale trade, banks, and transportation, which included the steamboats that brought smuggled alcohol upriver from Chicago or St. Louis. By 1876 he had the largest commercial enterprise in Benton and by 1881 one of the biggest in Montana.[35] Baker, too, became wealthy. In 1874 he formed a partnership with Charles and William Conrad, becoming I. G. Baker and Co.

One eye-witness observer in the Cypress Hills was Norbert Welsh. He recalled the trading season of 1875 in some detail. Welsh established his winter camp at Four Mile Coulee. He remembered stiff competition early in the year, mainly because the American companies were able to offer a wider selection goods than independent traders who tried to set up business. Prices paid for buffalo robes rose and competition was intense. Welsh said: "I tell you it was very hard now to get a robe from the Indians or half-breeds."[36] By the end of March, Welsh was prepared to head back to Fort Garry with his take of the season's trade and in spite of the competition he got his fair share. Welsh left the Cypress Hills with 120 good buffalo robes, 1,119 kilograms (3,000 lb) of pemmican, and 373 kilograms

(1,000 lb) of dried meat. He did not make it to Fort Garry and instead sold his goods to HBC Chief Factor Archibald MacDonald at Fort Ellice.

Welsh sold his horse for $175; the buffalo robes for $12 each; and the pemmican at 37 cents per kilogram (15 ¢/lb). In total Welsh left Fort Ellice with $600 for his pemmican and $1,400 for his robes. MacDonald had warned Welsh that prices at Fort Garry were low and he was right—when Welsh arrived at Red River robes were going for only $10 apiece. At Fort Garry Welsh took his remaining dried meat in trade goods and headed back for another season. Welsh was back out on the plains by July. He rested at Qu'Appelle then headed for Lebret. In August Welsh took a round trip of the prairies to trade for pemmican—a total of twenty days. During this time Welsh accumulated 1,865 kilograms (5,000 lb) of pemmican and dried meat, which he sold to HBC trader Isaac Cowie at 37 cents a kilogram (15 ¢/lb). He then took half in cash and half in trade goods and headed to his wintering place in the Cypress Hills. When Welsh reached his house he set to repairing it, mudding both his house and store-house. Welsh was set up ready to trade by the beginning of November. He was among the last of the Canadian free traders to operate in the Cypress Hills. By 1877–78 the independent trade in the region was over.

Some of the White traders have been romanticized and described as having the dignified-sounding qualities of "independence" and "self-respect," which were highly prized and praised both by contemporaries and later commentators. While the image of the rough and ready "Wild West" with its gunslinger hero dominates the popular imagination for these times, much of the so-called lawlessness extended from the commercial ethic to exploit the diminishing resources rather than from any inherent evilness on the part of the free traders. Some of Whoop-Up County's violence was the result of racial bigotry, especially toward Indians by those who hunted for wolves. The occupation of the plains by the Indians for hundreds of years could hardly be termed peaceful—they maintained alliances or fought for territory as the situation demanded, just as any European power would. But it was the idea of "lawlessness," of an "unpatroled" territory that was feared by Eastern politicians and their constituents, and they believed it needed to be brought under control.

Frontier violence, without a doubt, had grown, and Canadian officials saw the need to avoid at all costs an international incident that might lead to American annexation of the region. There was constant tension between the wolfers and the Cree, Assiniboin, and Blackfoot tribes, who were as well armed as their counterparts. It had been just one year earlier on April 5, 1872, that four Assiniboin had been massacred in the Sweet Grass Hills just south of the Cypress Hills in Montana. At least ten other Assiniboin were wounded when Thomas Hardwick led a group of wolfers in an unprovoked attack on a passing band of Assiniboin.

It has been assumed the independent traders that Baker and Power backed were American Civil War veterans, just recently out of uniform and prone to violence, or unemployed gold seekers eager to earn easy money by debauching the Indians with whiskey.[37] Some, but far from all, were Civil War veterans.[38] In general, those who worked at the whiskey trading posts in Canada can be divided into two classes: the traders and interpreters who had fur-trading experience in the previous decades, often with the AFC, and who actually dealt with the Indians, and the poorly paid hired men or *engagés*.

Some of the hired men had come to Montana after gold nuggets had been discovered in Grasshopper Gulch in 1861. They may have prospected but later found their hopes for wealth dim when the diggings played out after 1865. These men built the whiskey posts, chopped wood, and "wolfed." An examination of accessible biographical information indicates that people associated with this trade came from a wide variety of backgrounds—not only veterans but newcomers excited by the propsect of making money quickly along with experienced traders. Some of the key figures who were veterans of the Civil War were the wolfer Thomas Hardwick, as well as Charles and William Conrad. All three had served in the Confederate Army.[39] Two others are sometimes reported as having fought in the war, but J. J. Healy came West with the U.S. Dragoons in 1858 and D. W. Davis enlisted in the U.S. Army in 1867.[40] The whiskey trade was pushed forward both by restless veterans and also by experienced traders.[41] A large number of traders had worked for the AFC, including I. G. Baker, Alexander Culbertson, Joe Kipp, Alexis Labombarde, Jerry Potts, or for other trading companies, like William J. S. Gladstone, who had worked for the HBC and Abel Farwell, formerly with Durfee and Peck.[42]

American traders built at least forty-five trading locations, which included forts, posts, log shacks, sod huts, and dug-outs in southern Alberta and Saskatchewan.[43] Some traders did not construct even rudimentary shelters, but traded, mainly whiskey, directly out of wagons. In the Cypress Hills of Saskatchewan Cowie's HBC post, established in 1871, seems to have been the first in the area, and he reported later being joined by several free traders. Cowie left the site in the spring of 1871 and indicated he did not reoccupy it because of the American traders who had established themselves there during the summer.

On May 19, 1872, an Edward McKay, a Métis, and his wife, Caroline

Cook, established a trading post and farm on Battle Creek, just south of the later site of Fort Walsh.[44] Aided by two married sons and several hired men and their families, the McKays grew potatoes and barley, put up hay, and kept horses and cattle. They also hunted for buffalo and traded for robes with the Peigan, Nez Percé, and Crow in the Sweet Grass Hills, and with the local Cree, Assiniboin, and Métis. When the North-West Mounted Police arrived, the McKays remained as small traders and contractors, supplying the newly established Fort Walsh with buffalo meat, and later with beef, butter, milk, and cheese, and Edward carried the mail from Fort Benton. Two of their daughters married Mounties: Jemima married John Henry Grisham Bray, and Emma married Peter O'Hare. Edward died in 1884, and his body was eventually buried in Medicine Hat.

Father Jean-Marie Lestanc reported five or six trading posts in the Hills during the 1872–73 trading season. Only a handful of these are specifically known: the establishments of Abel Farwell and Moses Solomon, the post of man named "Genoa" near East End, and possibly the posts of Paul Rivers and William Rowe, and one Addison MacPherson.[45] It has been said, in the spring of 1873, there were thirteen traders within five kilometers (3 mi) of Little Soldier's camp in the Cypress Hills.[46] In November 1873, following the Cypress Hills Massacre, Lestanc indicated that no American forts remained. Four or five posts were re-established in the area in 1874, but the trade ended with the arrival of the NWMP the next year.[47]

Competition for access to the lucrative trade in buffalo hides was not limited to the individual free traders but sometimes also extended to violent attempts to force out rivals as both I. G. Baker and T. C. Power ruthlessly pursued profit. One confrontation between wolfers of the "Spitzee Cavalry" (derived from the Blackfoot word *aapi'si,* which means wolf), led by John Evans and Harry "Kamoose" Taylor, and the traders of Fort Whoop-Up was ostensibly over the guns the latter were supplying to the Indians. Headquartered at Fort Spitzee, near High River, Alberta, the members of the Spitzee Cavalry resented this trade since it made their own presence in the territory more dangerous. The Indians approved of the traders' presence in the territory but disliked the wolfers. Evans attempted to force traders to sign a declaration that they would no longer supply guns to the Indians. J. J. Healy, representing the T. C. Power Co., refused, and it became evident that the Spitzee Cavalry was, to a significant degree, representing the interests of William Conrad and the I. G. Baker Co. The confrontation with Healy was thus a thinly disguised attempt to drive him out of the territory to reduce the competition for Conrad's traders.

For the most part the trade in Whoop-Up Country was much less dramatic. American traders in the Cypress Hills, such as Abel Farwell, were occupied most of the time keeping books, trading, loading and unloading their wares, packing robes and furs, maintaining equipment and horses, hiring teams, dealing with freighters, and keeping up good relations with those who came to trade at the fort.

The start of the trading season was one of the busiest times of the year for the traders. During the summer they had made arrangements at Fort Benton to prepare for the approaching season. The trader would begin by bargaining to secure a contract with one of the large wholesale merchants in Fort Benton. Here his skills as a businessman would be tested as he negotiated for his consignment of goods. Many factors had to be taken into account in selecting the inventory for the season. The competition between Power and Baker meant that trading experience and knowledge of the territory were important for a trader going into the field. The traders transported a great variety of goods north from the Missouri, and not just staples but luxury items as well were demanded by their customers. There were basically three categories of goods: first, food and drink; second, hardware goods; and third, items of clothing and shoes.

The merchandising and warehouse interests of T. C. Power and I. G. Baker were formidable, and these merchants boasted they could supply their customers with any item that could be bought in New York. They sold everything from farm implements and mining supplies, to silk, fine cloths, liquor, cigars, and perfumes. But what eventually became of greater importance to both companies was the money made from securing large government contracts from either Washington or Ottawa. These lucrative government contracts provided goods to armies, police forces, and Indian agencies. It was important for these companies to have agents in the field. Traders like Farwell and Solomon represented the companies' interests in frontier areas, where a presence had to be maintained. The ability to supply goods anywhere there was a demand was paramount, and both organizations were well aware of this. Competing traders representing rival suppliers were often found in the same vicinity, whether they set up in the Cypress Hills or in the Alberta foothills.

The most necessary of the traders' supplies were food and drink. Beef was sometimes sold in cans, as corned beef, but the meat staples were salted, smoked, and dried bacon, carried out to the trading forts in sacks or in boxes. The other most common foodstuffs included flour, tea, and tobacco. But there were also a wide variety of other items: soda biscuits, baking powder, bran, cod-liver oil, dried apples, a variety of salted pork or ham, canned and powdered milk, pepper, rice, salt, and syrup. Other canned goods were carried as well: coffee, cranberries, salmon, beans, and oysters. Luxury items included jams and jellies, Worcestershire sauce, and pickles. Numerous so-called drugs were available, among them vanilla, strawberry, and raspberry extracts, Epsom salts, ginger root, and sulfur.

There was a large selection of tobacco available with brand names such as Flor de Canada, Laureate, Embema de Cuba, Traviata, Sara Bernhardt, Calipe, Reyna delor Mares, Variety Fairs, Briars, Gold Flake, Prince of Wales, and Napoleon. The traders also kept a wide variety of alcohol: English whiskey, Bourbon whiskey, regular whiskey, Hermitage whiskey, port wines, and brandy. For the Indians the traders usually created their own concoctions from raw alcohol, watered down with creek water, to which various ingredients were added.

Many hardware items were popular as trade objects: axes, gun ammunition, buckboards, bull rings, camp equipment, cartwheels, chains, chisels, churns, clocks, horse and ox collars, curry combs, knives, dishes, files, fish hooks, harness, harrows, hoes, lamps, matches, nails, kettles, plows, rakes, scales, scythes, screws, shovels, sleighs, snares, stoves, straps, spoons, tents, tool chests, twine, wagons, washboards, washtubs, wheelbarrows, wire wrenches, and yokes.

A wide array of men's and women's clothing was also for sale: vests, shawls, shoes, boots, shirts, pants, and dresses. Colorful cloths were very popular and many rolls of patterned material were sold each year. Leather goods, other than shoes, were also available in the form of jackets and coats. In addition, felt blankets, thread, ribbons, handkerchiefs and thimbles, guns, mirrors, playing cards, stationery, and kerosene rounded out the multitude of articles that were traded.

The most profitable item of all was whiskey. It was usually watered down and mixed with a variety of ingredients for taste. One standard recipe suggested adding red pepper, chewing tobacco, and molasses. Other more elaborate concoctions included Perry Davis Vegetable Painkiller, Dr. J. Hostetter's Stomach Bitters, Jamaica ginger, and red ink. The greed for quick profits fueled this unsavory trade. Though short in duration, great profits were realized extending right from the free trader in the Cypress Hills through to eastern American companies with their head offices in elaborate high rises in Chicago, St. Louis, and New York.

After bargaining and purchasing his goods in Fort Benton, the trader had one other major task to make ready for the fall trip to the frontier: to arrange for transportation. Complications sometimes arose since the traders were all in competition for the best teams. There can be little doubt that deals would be struck and favors paid in local saloons during the summer months in order to ensure reliable transport. With teams and wagons ready, bull whackers hired, the merchandise loaded, and hay for feeding the teams aboard, the trader would be ready for the weeks of travel northward, where he would set up for winter trade. The men that supplied the transport were often Métis, who had a long tradition of acting as tripmen for goods being brought into the territory and then taking the furs and robes back to the trade centers. This had been done for the HBC or NWC primarily by canoe or York boat, but the tripmen readily adjusted as the fur trade moved beyond the water routes and fur-trade goods were moved overland by mule and ox trains.

The trip from Fort Benton was a slow one, taking from three to four weeks depending on the weather and the size of the train. It would usually be made some time between late August and mid-September. This was still a season when there could be much torment from blackflies and mosquitoes, and a time when the weather could be unpredictable.

Upon arrival in the Cypress Hills in the fall, a site to establish trade would have to be chosen. The trader would need to keep an eye out for the proximity of game and water, and have a familiarity with the territory's inhabitants in order to select a spot favorable for trading. The trader might make use of a fort occupied the previous season. If it was in a usable state he would occupy it and begin repairs. But if he desired a new site, he would begin the process of gathering and preparing logs to begin construction. This activity would mean extra costs for the trader as the tripmen would then have to be kept on to help with the building of a structure that usually consisted of three or four cabins and a palisade. There could be a building for the trader and his family, one for the help that would stay with him through the winter, and another that would be the trading store. The palisade was for protection, and to keep those who had come to trade from milling around inside. Indeed, much of the trade that took place throughout Whoop-Up Country was through a hole in the fort's palisade or door. Worn rock and ruts from the wagon wheels of the long bull-trains can still be seen throughout the Cypress Hills area.

With the fort built and goods unloaded, the trader would hire one or two tripmen to stay with him throughout the trading season to assist with the trade and the maintenance and supply of the fort. The merchandise had to be organized and stored to ensure that spoilage would be minimal. Once the premises were in order, there would be time to spend fishing and hunting for food to carry the fort's inhabitants through the long winter months. Ducks and geese would be heading south during the fall season, and the opportunity to kill a moose or deer might present itself. Any game caught would be brought home and, in Farwell's case, prepared by his Crow Indian wife. Other work during this season would include making sure the roofs were watertight and the chinking was in place, to prevent the winter winds from whistling through the log walls. The traders were ready for the arrival of winter, awaiting the Cree and Métis to bring in their furs and buffalo robes. Winter evenings might be spent playing cards, reading, drinking, smoking, or in conversation with travelers.

As the business began, the traders would be occupied in exchanging goods for the furs, skins, and hides brought to the fort. Major tasks would include bargaining, evaluating furs, and bookkeeping. The season's trade would consist of the staple—the buffalo robe—as well as bear, lynx, marten, fox, beaver, wolf, coyote, skunk, badger, muskrat, antelope, deer, elk, and even gopher and rabbit. During the bargaining, the trader often relied on his wife or hired hands to speak with the Indians in their own language and dialect.

At the beginning of the season the Indians usually traded for the more substantial hardware and clothing goods offered by the trader. But as the winter season began, they would be forced to trade for food as their own supplies became exhausted. Tea, flour, and bacon were preserved until well into this season when the demand for them was highest. Alcohol was in greatest demand in the fall. In the 1870s, when stray buffalo were scarce in the Cypress Hills, the Indians became more dependent on goods available from these traders—and later from the NWMP—than they had been a decade earlier when food was more plentiful. As the buffalo disappeared there was also greater competition for other game in the region such as elk and deer, compounding the food scarcity. Food shortages during these later years of the trade in Whoop-Up Country ensured that profits for the traders remained high.

Toward the end of winter the traders began planning their return to Fort Benton with the season's gains. Bundles had to be made and the packing of leftover goods to be completed. Arrangements were made for transportation back south. These last preparations were made around the end of May or the beginning of June. There would be a final flurry of trading as the Indians sought to obtain desired goods before they left on the summer hunt and the traders tried to divest themselves of any remaining stock. It was at just this time in 1873, as Farwell packed up ready to leave, that the Cypress Hills Massacre took place. Packed, loaded, and set to go, the laden bull-train would set off when the roads were dry enough to allow travel. The trip back would take three to four weeks.

Once back in Fort Benton the trader again called on his business skills and instincts to negotiate with the mercantile companies for a good price for his robes and furs. To determine the profit, bookkeeping and an accounting of the winter's transactions would be completed. It was only then, for perhaps two months from mid-June to mid-August, that the trader would have a break to relax and enjoy the benefits of his labor. It was a grueling pace, but the trade in the Cypress Hills was short-lived. In the aftermath of the Cypress Hills Massacre the NWMP arrived to end the trade of whiskey in a territory that the Canadian government had left unpatrolled. With the arrival of the police, the border could no longer be so freely traversed nor could the wolfers poison on the Canadian side of the border. It was the end of Whoop-Up Country north of the 49th parallel, an era that was centered on whiskey traders as agents of freewheeling American capitalism.

Fort Walsh, 1878. For centuries, Plains Indians had traveled to the Cypress Hills in search of lodgepole pine for lodge poles and horse and dog travois. The once thickly treed hills close to Fort Walsh were quickly denuded once the Mounties arrived and used the wood to build the fort and for fuel. (Montana Historical Society, 947–451)

North–West Mounted Police, Fort Walsh. Mounties liked to be photographed with Aboriginal people or wearing Indian garb to show friends and family what the West was like. (Glenbow Archives, Calgary, NA–1535–1)

Left: *Blackfoot at Fort Walsh, circa 1878. The Cypress Hills marked the western limit of the territory of the Blackfoot Confederacy that included Peigan, Siksika, and Blood. They were in constant conflict with the Cree, especially in the 1870s and 1880s when they were in competition for the same dwindling buffalo herds.* (Glenbow Archives, Calgary, NA–790–2)

Below: *Big Bear's camp near the Cypress Hills, 1883. Big Bear came to the Hills with the hope of organizing the local Indian bands into a united front. In 1883 starvation produced conflict among his people, who were in desperate need of government rations, and he resigned himself to moving north onto a reserve.* (G. M. Dawson/National Archives of Canada, PA–050746)

Above: *NWMP Superintendent James Morrow Walsh, circa 1882. James Walsh is best known for his handling of Sitting Bull and the Dakota who arrived in Canada close to Wood Mountain. Some say he was removed from his position at Fort Walsh because his relationship with Sitting Bull was "too good."* (Glenbow Archives, Calgary, NA–1771–1)

Right: The Graphic, *New York, engraving of Sitting Bull in council at Fort Walsh, October 1877. The Terry Commission met with Sitting Bull to try to persuade the Dakota to return to the United States. During the meeting, Sitting Bull told the American representatives that they were "liars" and that the Dakota had no intention of leaving Canada.* (Glenbow Archives, Calgary, NA–5091–1)

Sitting Bull sought refuge in the Hills after defeating General Custer at the Little BigHorn. For the first part of his life, Sitting Bull was best known as a warrior, but by the time he arrived in Canada he had become a peace maker trying to protect his people. (Glenbow Archives, Calgary, NA-4452-4)

Cree at Maple Creek. The Cree used the Hills extensively, often ranging beyond them into Blackfoot country. At the time of the treaties, the Canadian government feared a large concentration of Cree in the Hills and disallowed reserves in the area. Nekaneet's band refused to leave and was eventually granted a reserve in the Cypress Hills in 1913, although they did not receive treaty benefits until 1975. (Glenbow Archives, Calgary, NA–2883–8)

Cree women at Fort Walsh. Cree women played a crucial role in helping their people survive severe times of want as the buffalo disappeared. They were especially resourceful in gathering berries and snaring small game to make up for this loss as their people moved on to reserves. (Glenbow Archives, Calgary, NA–2446–9)

CHAPTER 4

THE CYPRESS HILLS MASSACRE

The intensely competitive trade for buffalo robes and furs ultimately produced the volatile conditions responsible for the Cypress Hills Massacre of June 1, 1873. It was the theft of some horses from a party of American wolfers by Crees that set in motion the chain of events that culminated in the massacre of a group of Assiniboin a few weeks later in the Cypress Hills.

For the Assiniboin, led by Chief Manitupotis (Little Soldier), the winter of 1872–73 had been a hard one. Food supplies were becoming increasingly scarce for all who lived on the prairies. The Assiniboin had been camped with other bands by the Battle River when their food supplies ran out in February. Little Soldier's band believed their best hope would be to move south to the Cypress Hills, and so they began a 480-kilometer (300-mi) trek across the frozen prairie. During this "starving time," thirty band members died.

The band finally reached the shelter of the Hills in late winter. Game was more abundant there, and the people slowly began to regain their strength. They also hoped to trade with the Americans they knew to be wintering in the Hills. The Assiniboin remained there during the spring recovering from their ordeal, an experience they shared with many other plains people at this time. At the end of May 1873, the Assiniboin were camped in a beautiful valley alongside the north fork of the Milk River. There they were joined by another small band of Assiniboin under Chief Inihan Kinyen. It was traditional for plains tribes to join together in the spring in larger units to hunt the buffalo, something that was becoming increasingly difficult by the 1870s. The camps of Little Soldier and Inihan Kinyen together consisted of three hundred people, fifty of whom were soldier-warriors.

Close by the camp were two small log forts belonging to wintering White traders representing American companies from Fort Benton. On the west side of the creek was Abel Farwell's post and on the other side, a few hundred meters (yards) to the north-east, was that of Moses Solomon.

Abel Farwell (variations of this English surname include Farewell and Fairwell) was thought to have been born around 1842 in Massachusetts.[1] The heavy-set and rather tall Farwell may have been trained as a carpenter in the East, but by the 1870s he described himself as "a trader by occupation."[2] There is some evidence he traded for the HBC on the Mackenzie River, and he first clearly appears in the historical record in 1867 as the foreman that supervised the building of Fort Peck for the firm of Commodore E. H. Durfee and Colonel C. K. Peck. The fort was constructed on the Missouri River, close to the border between Montana and Dakota territories.

The stockade was about 300 feet [90 m] square with walls of 12 feet [4 m] high of cotton-wood logs set vertically, with 3 bastions and 4 gateways on front, and two bastions on the rear. Within were various log buildings including quarters for the men, storehouses, blacksmith shop, stables, corral and even a slaughter house.[3]

Fort Peck was operated as a trading post until 1871, dealing with the Assiniboin and Dakota, but Farwell only traded there that season and the next. In the fall of 1869, supplied by T. C. Power, he traded at an unknown location in northern Montana or Canada. Interestingly, that same year, Isaac Cowie mentioned that near Fort Qu'Appelle a trader appeared who could well have been Farwell: "An American from Fort Peck, on the Missouri, got among the Indians."[4] A year later it is thought that Farwell again came to Canada and established a post in southern Alberta on the St. Mary's River, just north of the U.S. border.[5] In 1871, he returned to the employment of Durfee and Peck and constructed Fort Belknap in the Milk River valley. He did not trade there, the post trader being Thomas M. O'Hanlon, but worked for Durfee and Peck at Clear Creek on the Marias River.[6]

By October 1871, Farwell had a new post in southern Alberta just above the Sweet Grass Hills. His activities there are an illustration of just how bitter the competition could get in the border trade. Farwell called in the American military because of rival John Kerler, a Canadian trader from Red River, who was with a group of Métis buffalo hunters. They were illegally trading whiskey on the U.S. side of the line near Frenchman's Creek, a small tributary of the Marias. Two companies of U.S. infantry duly destroyed Kerler's post in October or early November.[7]

By the fall of 1872 thirty-one-year-old Abel was a very experienced trader. That year he obtained his supplies from the T. C. Power Co. and built a trading post in the Cypress Hills. His fort consisted of a one-room cabin with a wooden floor and two adjoining areas with upright log walls that could have been dirt-floored rooms or stockaded enclosures. The whole structure was about thirteen meters (43 ft) long and four meters (14 ft) wide and was served by a single gate to the front. At least one cabin was attached to the rear of this structure.[8]

Some time before 1872, Farwell had married a River Crow woman originally named Goes First, known by this time as Horse Guard (although Whites often called her "Mary" or "Crow Mary"). Farwell's detractors later claimed he was at this time also married to a White woman, whom he never divorced.[9] Horse Guard was born about 1855 in southern Montana, daughter of Crooked Arm or Horse Guard, a Crow man, and his wife, Strikes Plenty Woman, a Gros Ventre he had taken captive into the Crow tribe.[10] Farwell may have met Horse Guard when her people came to Fort Benton to trade. "Mary" became his partner and assisted Farwell considerably with his trade.

Farwell had another partner that winter of 1872–73. This was George Leonard Hammond, born on May 17, 1842, at St. Leonard's, New Brunswick—although in the 1880 and 1900 U.S. censuses Hammond claimed he was born in Maine, probably to affirm his identification with the U.S.[11] His great-grandfather Archelaus Hammond had left the U.S. during the American Revolution and settled at Kingsclear, New Brunswick. The family prospered in their new home. Some fifty years later, George's father, A. B. Hammond, Sr., married Sarah Coombs, and then a year after her death in 1838, her younger sister, Glorianna. The Coombs sisters were also of Loyalist ancestry, and their father, Leonard Reed Coombs, had founded St. Leonard's. Sarah Hammond eventually gave birth to two girls and four boys. The lives of two of her male children— George and his younger brother Andrew Benoni, Jr. ("A.B."), both of whom left for the American West—were entwined.

George was educated in the public schools of New Brunswick and learned to speak fluent French from local Acadians. At the age of sixteen he left home, with A.B., for Bangor, Maine. The two boys had picked up the logging trade of their father, and they spent a couple of years in a logging camp in Maine before moving on to Williamsport, Pennsylvania, where they worked on the Susquehanna River. Some time in the early 1860s the two decided to "go West," and managed to get as far as St. Joseph, Missouri. In 1865, George parted company with A.B. and relocated in Montana Territory. He reached Fort Benton in 1867 on the steamer *Imperial,* and was joined shortly by his brother.[12] George obtained a contract to supply wood to the U.S. government from a woodyard on the Musselshell River, while A.B. remained at Fort Benton over the winter also working as a "woodhawk," and then left for Missoula in the spring of 1868. "Woodhawks" or "wood choppers" cut and stockpiled timber along the

Missouri to refuel the steamboats that plied the river. Many woodhawks also worked as wolfers in the winter months, and because of the animosity this created amongst local Indian people theirs could be a perilous occupation.[13] It was said that in one year in the mid-1860s, the Dakota killed fifty-eight wood choppers on the eastern side of Montana.

In 1867, according to Old Joe Butch, a Missouri woodhawk, George helped Farwell with the construction of Fort Peck.[14] In 1868, he moved to Helena and then to Missoula, where he rejoined his younger brother. George landed a job in Hell Gate, but a year later the pair were off once more, this time taking a herd of horses to Puget Sound, Washington. In early 1870, the two brothers were back in Montana with a herd of horses and while A.B. returned to Hell Gate, George chose to center his activities in Fort Benton.

In the 1870 census George Hammond was listed as working as a wood chopper at a woodyard below Fort Benton. Though based in Benton, he spent much of the next three years in Canada, involved in wolfing and the whiskey trade. His short biography in *Progressive Men of the State of Montana* indicates somewhat euphemistically that, at this time, he was involved in "merchandising."[15] In the fall he was among those, supervised by former HBC employee William Gladstone, who rebuilt Fort Whoop-Up, and following its construction he remained in southern Alberta wolfing and trading.[16] A year later, Hammond and his team of horses were members of the party led by Charles Rowe, an expedition that included in its number the infamous whiskey trader Fred Kanouse. The group of traders clashed with Indians on the Marias River and then built Fort Stide, sixteen kilometers (10 mi) downstream from Joe Kipp's Standoff Post on the Belly River.[17] When spring came Hammond moved on to the Highwood River area and joined up with the Spitzee Cavalry gang. He was with the group that challenged J. J. Healy for control of the local fur trade. By June, George was back in Benton where he sold his 380 buffalo robes, 67 buffalo calf robes, 201 wolf pelts, and 10 coyote pelts to T. C. Power for $2,796.[18]

In the 1872–73 trading season Hammond formed an association with Farwell, his old foreman from Fort Peck and a man he had been in contact with in Fort Benton. Hammond seems to have been a junior partner to Farwell. He obtained goods on credit from the senior trader and may have chopped wood and traded whiskey while Farwell worked on the accounts. Hammond may well have been the man the Assiniboin called Pahazzi (Blonde Hair)—a somewhat disliked trader who dispensed the watered-down liquor and who, although he could not speak their language fluently, knew it well enough to trade.[19] Where Hammond lived that winter is unclear. He may have stayed inside Farwell's Post, although the structure was none too large, or perhaps in a cabin close by with other traders and wolfers. With him lived a woman he was to marry in Fort Benton in 1874.[20]

His wife-to-be was Rosalie Wills, close to twenty years old by June of 1873. It is not known where they first met, perhaps in Fort Benton or possibly in the Cypress Hills that year. She was born August 1, 1853, probably in Manitoba, although later she, like her husband, indicated an American birthplace, in her case Minnesota.[21] In later years a Montana old-timer recalled she was "a very pretty woman. She had some Indian blood but not very much, just enough to make her attractive. Her girls were, too."[22] Rosalie had a very generous and kind personality and, unusual for a woman with her background, she could read and write English, no mean accomplishment considering she never had formal schooling.

Rosalie's people were Métis who had had a long association with the HBC and the fur trade. In Canada, on her paternal side, the family was begun by her great-great-grandfather John Favel, Jr., and his Swampy Cree wife, Titameg. Their grandson John Richards McKay, born in 1792, traded for the HBC in Manitoba. He married Harriet Ballenden, a woman seven years his junior, daughter of John Ballenden and his Indian wife, "Jane." John Richards and Harriet had sixteen children in all and among them were Edward McKay, the trader who established a post in the Cypress Hills in 1872, and Rosalie's mother, Mary McKay, who was born in 1820. She married John Wills, Jr., son of John Wills and Josephite Grant, on September 6, 1842. Together they had ten children, including Rosalie, and adopted one son, Alexander Wills, who was born in 1877 in the Cypress Hills.[23]

There were several additional people associated with Farwell that season. Foremost was Alexis Labombarde, a Métis hired to interpret for Farwell, and his wife, Nancy, who sewed and cooked for those at the post. Others did work not so skilled. They included James Marshall and Andrew Peterson, the latter born in Sweden and still wolfing in 1906. These two men lived in a cabin at the rear of Farwell's Post. Other, less distinct, figures associated with Farwell include a man named Kerr and Gary Bourke. Philander Vogle, who during that winter froze his feet, had been with Farwell on the journey north but later resided with Solomon. Precious little information is available on these men who "worked around gener-ally," doing jobs like chopping wood, shoveling snow, skinning animals, and baling furs for their boss Farwell, the chief trader.[24]

Two hundred meters (600 ft) to the east, on the opposite side of the creek, stood the post of tobacco-chewing Moses Solomon. He was said to have been a short, but strong man with a thin black mustache, light blue eyes, and good a sense of humor.[25] Forty-five years old in 1873, Moses Solomon (also Salomon or Soloman) was born the third child of a Jewish family in the village of Beerfelden, Germany, on August 15, 1828.[26] He received both a standard Jewish and a common education, and it is believed he apprenticed as an upholsterer before he left Germany at the tender age of seventeen. He arrived in New York City with his brother Sol in 1848.[27] Selling a stock of goods to pay their way, the pair reached the Peoria, Illinois, home of their sister Esther, who had previously immigrated to the U.S. Apparently Peoria offered Moses and Sol few opportunities so they soon left to join the gold rush to California. It was not to be the last time Moses was lured afield by the precious metal. Around 1855–57 he left California for a new gold rush and probably took ship from San Francisco to the mouth of the Columbia River and then traveled to Walla Walla, Washington, to share in the bonanza of the Idaho fields. Moses's exact movements are unknown, but it appears he followed the trail of gold from Walla Walla to Boise, Idaho, and finally to Alder Gulch, Last Chance Gulch, and Confederate Gulch, all in Montana Territory.[28]

Moses failed to strike it rich and in the fall of 1865 he decided to try a new venture. He left the gold fields and established a trading post sixteen kilometers (10 mi) north of Fort Benton, across the Marias River from present Loma, and near the spot where the previous spring Blood Indians had killed ten wood cutters.[29] Close to the same time, Moses opened a saloon in Fort Benton. For the next twenty-six years he was to base his numerous commercial activities at his Marias trading post. It consisted of two adjoining five-by-five-meter (16-x-16-ft) unpainted cottonwood cabins with the rear room serving as a living quarters and the front as the "Indian Room," in which Moses traded for buffalo robes with the Gros Ventre, who camped by the Marias. He also used the post as a base for buffalo hunting and a host of other wide-ranging activities and adventures.[30]

Moses Solomon's search for profitable business activities led him north up the Whoop-Up Trail and then to the Fisk Wagon Road, both of which passed within a few kilometers (miles) east and west respectively of his post on the Marias.[31] Moses had posts in Canada in 1870–71, 1871–72, and 1872–73. At least one season, probably 1870–71, he was at Fort Slide-Out, a post on the river bottom on the east side on the Belly River twenty kilometers (12 mi) upstream of its confluence with the Oldman River. One explanation of the post's unique name relates how, when a group of traders was warned by a Native of a possible attack by Blood Indians, a Dutch trader exclaimed they had better "slide-out."[32]

Possibly in 1871–72, and without a doubt in 1872–73, Moses traded for buffalo robes in the Cypress Hills. In the fall of 1872, he established a post on the east bank of the north fork of the Milk River. He obtained most of his trade goods from T. C. Power and Co., but also bought from his rival just across the creek, Abel Farwell. Moses's Cypress post seems to have closely resembled his post on the Marias River. It consisted of an L-shaped two-room cabin: in the front a five-by-five-meter (17-x-17-ft) Indian Room, and in the rear a five-by-four-meter (17-x-13-ft) wooden-floored living quarters. This post also included an attached square stockade that featured bastions. A space was cut out to watch the Indian Room and the gate was fastened with a "log chain."[33] This porthole and chain were clearly necessary as Moses did not enjoy as good a relationship with his customers as did Farwell.

With Moses, from Montana, came John C. Duval, a Métis from Fort Benton; George Bell, a veteran of the American Civil War; and Antonio Amei, from New Mexico. Also at the post were Philander Vogle, who had moved over from Farwell, and John McFarlane, a hunter. There were no women at this fort.[34]

By May 1873, the trading season was nearly over. On a Saturday late in the month, a train of ox carts arrived at Farwell's Post to haul his take of robes, pelts, and unsold stock back to Fort Benton. The owners or teamsters of the carts and wagons were mostly Métis from wintering camps some forty kilometers (25 mi) east of the post. The Métis had already been told of the tensions between the American traders and the Assiniboin, and they heard of them again when they arrived to start freighting. The Assiniboin had accused Solomon of cheating them and had fired shots into his post. They threatened to "clear out" the traders and kill them all if they resisted.

Farwell was on better terms with the Indians than Solomon but this spring there appeared to be a general tension, perhaps due to the many plains peoples in competition for diminishing resources. At least one Assiniboin worked for Farwell and other Indians had helped him recover horses stolen by a passing party. One of the stolen horses had belonged to George Hammond. Other events in the Hills also contributed directly to the tense atmosphere. There had been a skirmish nearby between some Blackfoot and Assiniboin, and a couple of months earlier Indians had reportedly killed a trader just to the west of the trading posts, in present-day Alberta. These incidents—and the increasing presence of Whites, who searched farther and farther afield for diminishing animal resources of the area—produced hostility and suspicion between Natives and Whites.

The tension between the Assiniboin and Solomon might have ended without incident had it not been for events that had taken place two weeks earlier in Montana. A group of about a dozen wolfers were returning with their season's take and were only a day's journey from Fort Benton, when forty of their horses were stolen. Their large number of animals had not been closely guarded as the wolfers had not expected a raid on their camp so close to Fort Benton.

Some of this gang were the curs of the plains. Their leader was Missouri-born Thomas Hardwick, alias The Green River Renegade, who had been wounded three times with the Confederate Army. Although he married a Blackfoot woman, Close Kill, Hardwick had the reputation of being an Indian hater and was involved in the 1875 lynching of two Indian men in Fort Benton. Second-in-command was John H. Evans, also an American Civil War veteran. He had been a captain in the Montana Militia in 1867 and was one of the leaders of the Spitzee Cavalry. The year before, Hardwick and many of the men in the Spitzee Cavalry had been involved in a fight with Assiniboin known as the "Sweet Grass Hills Massacre." As a group, these wolfers were later referred to as "persons of the worst class in the country."[35]

After noticing that their horses were missing, Hardwick and his men attempted to give chase, but recognizing the futility of pursuit, headed for Fort Benton instead. Here they cashed in their furs and tried to organize a posse. There was little sympathy for them among local law officials, so they set out to find the thieves themselves, armed with their own ideas of frontier justice. They were, however, unable to follow the trail of the Cree who had taken their horses and, after a two-week chase, they were forced to admit the trail had gone cold. Those Cree had in fact headed toward Fort Whoop-Up in southern Alberta, but the wolfer party had headed the other way, east into the Cypress Hills.

The wolfers arrived in the Hills on the last day of May. They searched for their horses, but Farwell assured them Little Soldier's band was poor with very few animals of their own. The gang spent the evening drinking with the recently arrived Métis freighters. Having no particular business the next day, they began this again early in the morning, with Solomon joining in the festivities. There is little doubt that activity was well advanced by noon and that the Assiniboin across the creek were also drinking. In this atmosphere it was easy for the wolfers to direct their anger to another group, even though the Assiniboin had no connection with the original theft. The wolfers may simply have been looking for any excuse for a fight, and on the frontier where many Whites believed "that the only good Indian was a dead one," little provocation was needed.

Chief Inihan Kinyen was at Farwell's Post when the wolfers arrived that morning. Someone had warned him that the newcomers might make trouble, so when he returned to the encampment he suggested that the two bands take down their lodges and leave. His suggestion was ridiculed by Wincanahe, who along with some others was consuming the whiskey they had been given in return for Hammond's horse. A young Indian eyewitness, Eashappie, later recalled: "That morning whiskey flowed like water in the camps and by mid-day the tribesmen were all hopelessly drunk." Both chiefs, Little Soldier and Inihan Kinyen, were among them.[36]

The wolfers and traders exchanged tales of atrocities committed by Indians, and as they continued to drink they became progressively more belligerent. Around noon the situation reached a climax when Hammond's horse went missing for a second time. Cursing in both English and French, he began shouting that the Assiniboin had stolen it back—suggesting that they believed they would be rewarded with more whiskey if they returned it once more. Hammond went across to Solomon's and asked the wolfers to join him in seizing some Assiniboin horses in retaliation. These men needed little encouragement. They grabbed their rifles and proceeded toward the Assiniboin camp along with some Métis freighters, all of them sodden with drink. Alexis Labombarde in the meantime had discovered that Hammond's horse had only wandered off and shouted this to the men rushing toward the Assiniboin camp. Unfortunately it was too late; by this time there were few level heads willing to listen.

It is difficult to be certain what happened from that point on. Farwell later said that he tried to dissuade the angry men from becoming violent, and when this failed he waded across the river to the Assiniboin camp. He claimed that there he found an Assiniboin headman and concocted a deal in which he would take two Assiniboin horses as security until the missing horse could be found. Farwell knew little or no Assiniboin but swore afterwards that he had made himself understood and that the headman had agreed. About then, a Métis ran across to the camp to warn the Assiniboin of the approaching danger. People began to run from the camp.

As some of the Indians spoke to Farwell, Hammond attempted to take two horses from the Assiniboin but was stopped by Bighead, an armed warrior. Hammond returned to the wolfers and some of the freighters, who by this time had lined the edge of a coulee that faced the exposed Assiniboin camp on two sides. From the protection of the bush surrounding the coulee, these men were virtually unseen. Fearing the worst, Farwell told the Assiniboin to scatter. Then, according to his own testimony, he went to speak to the wolfers and tried to find Labombarde, who by this time had recovered Hammond's horse—but it was too late.

Somebody, possibly Hammond, fired a shot. The indiscriminate fire at the unprotected Assiniboin camp began. With Winchester and Henry repeating rifles, the men in the sheltered coulee fired volley after volley into the camp. The Assiniboin tried to fight back, but having few modern weapons, it was hopeless. Men, women, and children fled from the camp. Most headed for some timber fifty meters (yards) or so to the east; others hid in the bushes lining the coulee or crossed the river. Many were shot as they fled, including Inihan Kinyen. From distant cover the Assiniboin attempted to return fire, but this was to no avail.

The attackers then split up. One group recrossed the river to fire on the Assiniboin hidden at the mouth of the coulee. They were stopped by Assiniboin gunfire. The other group, according to Labombarde, "pushed into the tents or lodges," with the Benton men firing at the camp as they went. He then saw them drag four women and a man out of their lodges. The man was Little Soldier and one of the women was the chief's mother-in-law. Two years later she told what happened: "When I and my daughter were leading her husband [Little Soldier] to the Fort he saw his father dead. He threw up his arms and . . . turning to them he said: 'White men, you will know what you have done today. You never knew a Woody Mountain Assiniboin Indian to harm a white man.' . . . At that moment he was shot through the heart by one of the party of Americans."[37]

The women were then led away to Solomon's fort. The attackers were not content merely to kill the chief. According to Farwell and Labombarde, Little Soldier's head was cut from his body and raised on a lodge pole. That some such mutilation occurred was later confirmed by an Assiniboin who had witnessed the scene. After raising their grisly trophy, the men set about looting and destroying the camp.

Late in the afternoon some Assiniboin were seen moving on the hills behind Farwell's. Hardwick and four others immediately set off on horseback to attack them. As they approached the river, Ed Legrace was shot dead by a warrior concealed at the mouth of the coulee. Hardwick's party then retreated to the shelter of Solomon's Post. Thus the fighting ended. But the wolfers continued their orgy: some Assiniboin women were sexually assaulted throughout the night by S. A. Harper, John Evans, and Joseph Lange, a Métis freighter. Little Soldier's wife later told how she and others were repeatedly assaulted. None expected to live.

An Assiniboin recalled returning to the campsite: "After dark I went into the camp and saw a women with her back broken; she was still alive and was trying to move but could not. It was very dark. That was all I saw."[38] Later some Assiniboin returned to the site to gather their possessions. "The whole forty lodges started off, carrying everything on our backs, all our dogs having run off. We started in the night for the end of the mountain, to the halfbreeds [the Métis winterers' camp], they treated us kindly, giving us dogs, kettles and other things."[39] The Cypress Hills Massacre was over. It is still uncertain how many people died in the attack, but at least twenty are thought to have perished.

The next day traders at both Solomon's and Farwell's hastily finished packing. The wolfers agreed to stay until this was done and occupied themselves by burning the remains of the Assiniboin camp. Showing the strength of her character, Horse Guard obtained the release of four of the captive women from Solomon's Post.[40] There Ed Legrace was buried that morning under one of the floors within the stockade. The traders then pulled out and the wolfers rode off to continue the search for their missing horses. As they left, someone doused Solomon's Post with coal oil and set fire to it. Farwell's Post too burnt to the ground, work of the departing traders or later the infuriated Indians. The valley was left deserted except for the dead Assiniboin, who still lay where they had fallen.

AFTER THE MASSACRE

News of the Cypress Hills Massacre did not reach Ottawa until late in August 1873. The government soon initiated steps to have those involved extradited from the United States and tried for murder. The case languished for a time and then was taken up by the newly created NWMP. Five wolfers were arrested and brought before an extradition commission in Helena in July 1875. Farwell was the chief witness for the prosecution, and much of the defense's case was to claim that he was a liar. The wolfers claimed it was Farwell who led them to the Assiniboin camp, that their intentions were entirely peaceful, and that they had only fired when fired upon. As it turned out the prosecution's case was not strong enough and the wolfers were released. Soon afterwards, two traders and a wolfer were arrested in Canada and tried in Winnipeg in June 1876. Once again the government case was weakened by insufficient or contradictory evidence, and the three men were acquitted. The case was finally dropped in 1882 when it was apparent that no new evidence would be brought to light. The Mounties did not get their men.

There can be little doubt about with whom the blame for the actual fighting rests. As the American Commissioner, W. E. Cullen, said at the extradition hearing at Helena—although the "preponderance of testimony is . . . to the effect that the Indians commenced the firing . . . they were doubtlessly provoked to this by the apparently hostile attitudes of the whites. . . . An armed party menacing their camp, no matter for what purpose, was by no means a slight provocation."[41]

While the killing may not have been premeditated, there can be no excuse for its wantonness; however, this can be explained. The Assiniboin were victims of racial prejudice and the General Phil Sheriden frontier philosophy of shooting first, especially when it came to Indians. The Cypress Hills Massacre demonstrated the vulnerability of life, especially Native life, on the Canadian frontier.

CHAPTER 5

FORT WALSH AND THE MOUNTIES

The Cypress Hills Massacre had made it clear there was a need for some
kind of Canadian presence or authority for the region. Plans had already
been laid to form a paramilitary police force similar to the Royal Irish
Constabulary established by the British government to exercise its authority over Ireland. The force was to be given broad powers to both enforce
and administer the law. It was to prevent violence from breaking out—for
no better reason than that the young nation simply could not afford
expensive military campaigns to deal with internal or international disputes. The border had to be protected and the whiskey trade controlled. The
March West showed this task would not be easy. Preserving peace and
preventing crime sounded eminently sensible, even necessary, in May of
1873 when the Act of Parliament establishing the force was passed; in
practice the natural environment proved as difficult to overcome as the
lawbreakers the police pursued to ensure a peaceful Canadian West.

On July 8, 1874, three hundred Mounted Police left Fort Dufferin,
Manitoba, their temporary headquarters, and headed for the territories they
were to patrol. The NWMP dressed in scarlet, in the best British tradition, to
distinguish themselves from the blue of the American cavalry.

The hazards of the trail soon became evident. Water was frequently
scarce. After ten days of travel the original three-kilometer (2-mi) line of
the contingent had stretched to sixteen (10 mi). There were occasions when
as the advance guard pulled out in the morning, the last of the caravan pulled
into camp. Wagons breaking down as they moved across difficult terrain
were the single greatest cause of delay. During hold-ups tired, hungry oxen
would eat their harnesses of buckskin and collars stuffed with hay, which
in turn caused further delay. Had it not been for the hiring of Pierre Léveillé
and five other Métis early into the journey to assist, the police might never
have reached their destination.

The March West itself has been exaggerated and raised to the level of
mythology. The sacrifice and bravery of the police have been used to
present the NWMP as the harbingers of civilization to the Northwest. As is
evident from the Mounties' own reports, the March was a disaster even by
the standards of the day. White missionaries in the territories at the time

were amused by the scores of laudatory accounts of the painfully slow and blundering move across the plains.

During the winter of 1874–75 the troops of the NWMP were spread across the West from Winnipeg to the Rockies. They had marched first to southern Alberta, where indiscriminate whiskey trading had been taking place. The Mounties were still concerned about reports of whiskey trading activities in the Cypress Hills and plans included construction of a substantial fort in the Hills under the direction of Supt. James Morrow Walsh. The forts strung across the Canadian prairies during the first winter included Winnipeg, Dufferin, Fort Ellice, Swan River Barracks, Fort Qu'Appelle, Fort Edmonton, Wood Mountain, and Fort Macleod. Fort Macleod, with 16 officers and 140 men, was by far the largest.

In the spring, Walsh had traveled to Sun River, Montana, for fresh mounts and under favorable circumstances had set out for the Cypress Hills. Under the direction of scout Jerry Potts, Walsh's troop reached its objective, the Cypress Hills Massacre grounds, on June 7. A site for the fort was chosen some distance away from the killing ground in a flat area that had been cleared of underbrush by one of the frequent prairie fires that swept through the Hills. There was no difficulty finding timbers in the great stands of pine and spruce that grew throughout the Hills. The ground chosen was close to a creek of clear water that wound through the hilly terrain. Métis sawmen were soon busy cutting planks in the sawpits, while ax men prepared the hand-hewn logs that would serve as walls. The layout of the fort was similar to other small forts built throughout North America and closely modeled on Fort Macleod, constructed the previous fall. Stakes driven into the ground marked out the perimeter of the fort while some building exteriors served as part of the walled exterior. The buildings faced inward onto a square or parade ground.

A 3.5-meter (12-ft) stockade was erected by placing heavy logs 1.2 meters (4 ft) into the ground in trenches and packing earth and stones to secure them. The stockade was then plastered with mud and whitewashed. The walls of the stockade were reinforced around the top by driving square timbers onto the logs 1 meter (3 ft) from the top. The stockade enclosed an area of 95.7 meters (314 ft) east and west along the north side, 90.8 meters (298 ft) on the south side, 72.8 meters (239 ft) north and south on the east side and 58.5 meters (192 ft) along the west side. There were two bastions: one at the northwest corner and another, built later, on the southeast corner. These helped cover the approaches from the north and east. A main gateway opened to the east toward the main road to Fort Benton. Two main gates of equal strength swung into the fort from heavy iron hinges. When shut, the gates were held secure by heavy wooden crossbars, logging chains, and padlocks. Another gate opened to the creek on the west.

With an abundance of good timber available, the construction of a large number of buildings proceeded rapidly. From the southeast corner, going northeast, west along the northwest and south toward the southwest, the original buildings stood as follows: Superintendent's Residence or Walsh's Quarters, Officers' Mess, Sergeants' Mess and Quarters, Magazine, Stable No. 2, Sick-Horse Stable, Blacksmith and Carpenter's Shop, Stable No. 1, Cookhouse and Bakery, Barrack Rooms, and the Sergeant Major's Quarters. In the center of the square stood a Guardroom as well as two Quartermasters' Stores. There were no wooden floors built into the structures when they were first erected. Twelve-meter (40-ft) logs were cut for the walls of the fort buildings. At the end they were fitted "saddle back" or "square notched" for placement on top of each other. The roofs for these log-walled buildings consisted of slender poles laid down along a central ridge pole and supported by two "stringers." These poles were placed close together and covered with clay. Later improvements to the roofs included the placement of boards that were nailed to cross pieces that overlapped ("board and batten" roofing). Still later whip-sawn lumber was nailed inside along the walls and roof, and plank floors replaced the earth underfoot. The logs were whitewashed with clay taken from the Whitemud Coulee, just a few kilometers (miles) south of the fort.

A tall flagpole stood between the main gate and the Commissioner's Residence, built in 1878 for Commissioner James. F. Macleod when he made Fort Walsh the headquarters for the NWMP. A sundial was placed close to the flagpole and read daily by the trumpeter to determine the proper time for Reveille, Retreat, and Lights Out. Any Indians and Métis in the fort were expelled each day at sundown. Bunks for the men were built along the walls with round, white poplar poles; mattresses consisted of gunny sacks filled with hay. Windows for the building had been hauled by bull-train from Fort Benton and Helena. Latrines stood just outside the southwest bastion of the stockade. In 1879, a well was sunk between the Guardroom and the west gate. The fort was completed by the fall, largely thanks to the assistance of the local Métis workers.

The fort was run on a strictly military routine. The gates were locked at Retreat and not opened again until Reveille unless a patrol was leaving or entering—on such occasions it was opened by the sergeant in charge of the guard—or when a civilian or Indian sought entry—on such occasions the gate was opened under survey of the officer of the day. Fort Walsh and Fort Macleod were the two major forts situated to patrol the international boundary from the Rocky Mountains to Winnipeg. This was accomplished by establishing smaller outposts from the main fort. Four subposts were to be built around Fort Walsh: Wood Mountain, East End, Pinto Horse Butte, and Milk River (Kennedy's Crossing), with summer camps at Four Mile and Ten Mile coulees. Patrols were important as parts of the Cypress Hills were still significant gathering points for Indians and Métis hunters. In the 1870s Métis buffalo hunters still wintered in simple dwellings at places such as Four Mile Coulee.

True to military tradition, the routine of the police resembled that of an army. The changing of the guard is a good example. Patrols entering and leaving the barracks rode at attention and gave eyes right or left when passing the flagpole hoisting the Union Jack. NWMP funerals were accompanied by the gun carriage in the military tradition with customary graveside volleys. This was as the creators of the Mounted Police, a true paramilitary outfit, intended. Mounted and foot drill, artillery drill, saber and lance drill were all carried out in military fashion. Visitors such as U.S. general A. H. Terry were honored with full military trappings when they visited the fort. When Indian leaders from surrounding tribes arrived for official meetings, sentries were posted and the sentry at the gate presented arms. On unofficial visits an orderly accompanied requests to the officer commanding.

The ordinary routine of the fort was undramatic and perhaps this explains the high desertion rate from the force in the early years. An average day began with the orderly recording the weather: "Freezing very hard," "Weather frosty," "Thaw set in and temperature rose 25°." The morning would then be taken up with

Revielle	6:30 A.M.
Stables	7:00–8:00 A.M.
Breakfast	8:15 A.M.
Office	10:00 A.M.
Parade	10:30 A.M.
Stables	11:30 A.M.–12:30 P.M.
Dinner	1:00 P.M.

Afternoons included various drills and fatigues, among which would be carbine-revolver drill, barracks inspection, riding school, shingling stables and buildings, as well as other repair "fatigues." An ordinary afternoon would be divided into

Guard Mounting	1:45 P.M.
Parade	2:00 P.M.
Tea	4:30 P.M.

Stables	4:45–5:30 P.M.	
Retreat	4:45 P.M.	
Picquet Mounting	5:30 P.M.	
Night Guard	5:30 P.M.	
First Post	9:30 P.M.	
Last Post	10:00 P.M.	
Lights Out	10:15 P.M.	

Food was also monotonous and the plain daily diet of the men may have contributed to their boredom.

	lbs	oz	grams
Beef or Bacon or Pemmican	1	8	681
Flour	1	4	568
or Bread	1	8	681
or Biscuit	1	4	568
Potatoes	1	4	568
or Beans	1	4	568
or Dried Apples		2	57
Tea		½	14
Coffee		½	14
Sugar		3	78
Salt		½	14
Pepper		$1/36$	1
Rice		1	26

Time in the evening might be spent in the music room listening to concerts or singing songs or reading the wide variety of material that was available at the fort. A considerable amount of reading material was ordered at all NWMP posts. Legal statutes and texts were, of course, a necessary part of any officer's library. Any number of contemporary books and magazines might also have been found in Assistant Commissioner A. G. Irvine's bedroom; since such material was so important "to while away" time, especially in winter.

A number of books were known to have been at Fort Walsh. Among them were books by Marryat, Ainsworth, Bulwer Lytton, Cooper, Thackery, Lever's novels, Dickens, Samuel Lover, Sir Walter Scott, and James Grant. A large number and variety of magazines and newspapers were also present at Fort Walsh including *Canadian Militia Gazette, Grip, Seasides, Cosmopolitan, Lippincott, Family Library Quarterly, Chambers Journal, Capells Magazine, All the Round, Canadian Monthly, Sunday Magazine, Canada Farmer, The Field, Scientific American, Young Men of Great Britain, Le devoir Canadien, Le courier de Montréal, The Dominion*

Monthly, The Saskatchewan Herald, The Mail, and other eastern newspapers.

Games were another means of passing the long hours of winter. While many outdoor games were played in summer, such as cricket, tennis, croquet, and soccer, indoor games were more common in winter. Undoubtedly these indoor games would have been kept in the Commissioner's Residence, perhaps in Irvine's sleeping quarters. Billiard tables were known to be located at a number of NWMP posts and other games were played such as cards, and also bagatelle, backgammon, chess, draughts, and dominoes.

Distances on the prairies were immense and duties consisted primarily in patrolling large empty expanses. Fort Macleod was 320 kilometers (200 mi) to the west and Fort Benton, where the mail run was, was 288 kilometers (180 mi) south. Fort Benton was also where the Mounties obtained their supplies, where the banking was done, and the location of the nearest telegraph.

When Commissioner James F. Macleod, successor to the first commissioner of the NWMP, George A. French, made Fort Walsh his headquarters in 1878, it had 139 men and was by far the largest fort of the five that existed at that time. With the presence of Sitting Bull in the Fort Walsh area that year, the percentage of the force's men at the fort was 42 percent, but by 1881 it was down to 33 percent, and in December 1882 it had fallen to 27 percent. By the time the detachment was moved to Maple Creek, it was only 11 percent.[1] Other forts in existence at the time were Fort Macleod, Fort Calgary, Fort Edmonton, and Fort Battleford.

The arrival of the NWMP may have signified the end of the whiskey trade but not of commerce. In fact a different trade began to flourish with the Mounties, still along the north-south axis, and as before with American-based companies as the prime suppliers. The Mounties made their first contact with the Americans on their March West. As the Mounties plodded onward, they ran into numerous obstacles: floods, snowstorms, stampeding horses, and men unprepared for the hardships encountered. By the fall of 1874, they still had not made the progress anticipated. With winter approaching, the police were desperate for shelter. They sought and were given refuge at Fort Benton. Here Commissioner G. A. French, Macleod's predecessor, forged a friendship with I. G. Baker that was to last for many years. This relationship would reap significant dividends for the American merchants. Contracts won by them, sometimes in the face of equal bids from Canadian firms, would help to pull the Montana merchants out of the depression in which they had found themselves after the decline of the buffalo-robe trade.

The obvious choice for providing the police with supplies was the HBC. For a variety of reasons, however, the HBC was unable to establish itself effectively as an alternate supplier. Charles John Brydges, land commissioner for the Company from 1879–89, wrote that the influence of the I. G. Baker and the T. C. Power companies was preventing the HBC from securing contracts. Although Brydges laid the blame for this on bribery on the part of the I. G. Baker Co., he quietly admitted in his correspondence that the Company, at least in the early years, did not have the capacity to supply goods to the NWMP. It was most convenient, in any case, to have supplies brought through a system that was already established. In these early years, when survival was the predominant consideration, economic nationalism was rarely mentioned and sentiments favoring loyalty to Canadian companies fell on unsympathetic ears. Only the prime minister, Sir John A. Macdonald, lent consideration to such arguments and was able to wield his influence in some cases.

The value of contracts awarded by the Canadian government was considerable. In 1880 contracts amounting to $100,000 were up for tender; in 1881, $400,000; in 1882, $500,000—all very substantial injections into a frontier company, substantial enough to warrant bribery on the part of I. G. Baker to ensure that his company secured the contracts. The HBC was eager to move into the commercial retail trade and to diversify its traditional reliance on the fur trade. In 1880 Brydges wrote to London:

> The entire change which is about to take place in the position of the Mounted Police and the Indian Department in the North-West, affords the company a very favorable opportunity of obtaining a very large share indeed of that trade. If the opportunity is not taken advantage of this year, it will pass into the control of other parties.[2]

Brydges' fears were well founded, for the competition and the presence of Baker did affect the fur trade "by allowing Stobart, Eden and Co., Baker and others, to get hold they have of the general trade in certain districts, they are becoming powerful competitions in the fur trade, considerably reducing the profits of that trade. A good many of the officers realize this fact now."[3] Baker exercised an influence over the Canadian-based company Stobart, Eden and Co. This allowed Baker in some cases to avoid paying tariffs on goods coming directly from the United States. Through this Canadian subsidiary, Baker had a virtual monopoly on the lucrative contracts made available from the Canadian government.

The HBC, however, received political assistance in getting established from "Sir John," as Brydges referred to him. Unlike the NWMP, who continued to award contracts to American merchants, Macdonald, at least in this case, was motivated by a feeling of nationalism. As Brydges explains: "Our tenders Sir John told me, were about $50 in aggregate higher than Baker's, but he gave it to us because he did not want the Americans in. He wishes we would next year tender for every place and then, we would shut out Baker altogether because of his paying bribes to Smith and Kavanaugh."[4]

The influence of I. G. Baker lasted until 1891, when the I. G. Baker Co. sold its business and merchandise in the North-West Territories and real estate in Alberta to the HBC. Before the disappearance of Baker from the prairies, and while American merchants were still enjoying a virtual monopoly in the North-West, Fort Walsh retained a significant position in the operations of the police. More importantly in terms of material culture, the Mounties bought most of their goods south of the border. Indeed, even when the NWMP moved to Maple Creek, the T. C. Power store relocated with them. The relationship was in effect a *quid pro quo* whereby T. C. Power supplied the police with goods and in return the police provided these merchants with protection.

Before the NWMP arrived there was no significant or permanent retail trade in the Cypress Hills area: there was simply no stable population or demand to risk establishing this sort of commercial enterprise. Then, with the presence of the federal government in the form of the NWMP, survey parties, and the Indian Department, a new economic order was established, characterized by a heavy dependence by the local merchants on the business provided by government agencies. The government agencies attracted Indians and Métis, who became a prime market for the merchandise of the retail merchants. Even though the economic flow of goods remained through the north-south axis between Fort Benton and Fort Walsh, the primary cultural influence was eastern Canadian. Despite this, distribution from the east was still too arduous and the cost of obtaining supplies exclusively through Canada was prohibitive in both time and money.

A town rapidly grew up around the police fort, partly because of the protection the fort offered but primarily because of the market the policemen presented. As a result of the police presence, many Indians and Métis were also drawn into the area. Some came for protection and rations, but most came to collect their annuity payments. As Marsh, a merchant in the area, often observed in his letters to Fort Benton, "The money spent by the Indians [their annual treaty] will amount to about $12,000."[5] Goods sold to the Indians and Métis included blankets, clothing, shoes, food, and tobacco, as well as items considered luxuries, like mirrors.

The character of the town that sprang up around Fort Walsh in the late nineteenth century resembled a ramshackle shanty-town. Buildings were strewn in the Battle Creek valley in no apparent order. They represented an unconscious structural response in an environment where survival was still the primary consideration. As Wallace Stegner has written, this primal motivation results in a deceptively practical appearance: "People on a frontier revert quickly except when they are preserving some nicety, to folk skills, and some of these are so primitive that they seem to have scarcely any national character at all."[6] The function of most of the buildings reveals that the town was essentially a warehouse center. While the local laundry, the restaurant, and the hotels provided essential services, the pool halls and the local tailor could satisfy hedonistic or fashion desires.

The police investigated many crimes at Fort Walsh, but the most sensational concerned the death of Constable Marmaduke Graburn, who was shot in a coulee just to the west of the fort on November 17, 1879. Graburn was found shot through the back of the head at a campsite to which he had returned to retrieve an ax. From the beginning, the police were convinced that Graburn was shot by member of a band of Blood Indians who had camped in the vicinity some days previously. The evidence used to connect the suspect, Star Child, to the crime was, even in the beginning, slim at best. Regardless, Star Child was doggedly pursued until he was apprehended two years later. The police could hardly be accused of impartiality in the conduct of their investigation. In the police reports Star Child was described as "a particularly insistent mendicant—a pinched-faced, evil eyed Indian of small stature, who, while given to profuse self-praise and boastfulness; was not above eking out a livelihood by sheer beggary."[7] But even such demonizing imagery was not enough to convict Star Child. Two years after the killing, not even a jury of six Albertan ranchers who heard the evidence against Star Child at Fort Macleod could convict him.

That there might have been other, perhaps even White, suspects, even fellow Mounties, that should have been investigated apparently never occurred to the police. If there was any doubt about the perpetrators of frontier crimes it seems clear that the police always looked for their man among the "regulars" they seemed perpetually to be "rounding up." Thus the process of hegemony, of imposing Anglo-Canadian standards on "the lesser breeds" seen as being without the law, in part explains the confidence of the police in pursuing their duties as vigorously as they did, even in instances where caution might have been better advised. A sense of mission was rarely lacking in paramilitary forces like the NWMP. After all, the force was modeled after British examples that were so effectively used throughout the empire.

CHAPTER 6

TREATIES AND RESERVATIONS

In the early 1870s, as the buffalo herds diminished, the Cree had no choice but to turn to the Canadian government in Ottawa for assistance—a government that was offering to settle them on reserves in return for title to their lands. Some turned to agriculture to try to alleviate starvation, but crop failure and government regulation were to make these attempts difficult. More frequently, Indians sold furs to independent American traders who had established their posts across the southern Canadian prairies. Some of these traders, and the commercial concerns that had backed them, remained and continued their trade in these territories even after the arrival of the NWMP, but the Indians were finding fewer and fewer hides and pelts to trade with them. Their options for survival were running out as Sir John A. Macdonald's National Policy, with its aim of a West settled by Euro-Canadians, closed in on them.

What is clearly evident from the life of the Cree at this time is that they remained a functioning and vital people. As historians Arthur Ray and John Milloy point out, they were never directly the victims of Europeans or other Indians, but consciously and rationally adjusted to new circumstances.[1] However, through the years their condition increasingly presented them with new problems. Milloy especially emphasizes that by 1870 the Cree were not destitute but were as powerful as they had ever been and were in a strong position to meet any challenges put to them. They had an enviable military and diplomatic record as they faced the Canadian state that was moving westward. In the past they had often faced new economic and military situations and had come through each crisis: from their life as woodland Indians, to the first contact with Europeans, from their adaptation to the gun and horse, to their role as middlemen in the fur trade when they traded with White and Indian alike, and finally as plains buffalo hunters. All of these changes had not dramatically affected their internal social dynamic.

In the eyes of Euro-Canadians, the ironic tragedy for the Indians in the 1880s was not their new dependence on the Whites but that they had not internally changed to become a materialistic, accumulating people. Such a change would have facilitated their adaptation to the capitalistic society in which they now had to live. They had outlived the buffalo on the plains and the spiritual strength derived from this close contact with nature was now more distant as they settled on reserves. What had served them so well for hundreds of years would now be a hindrance. "What was led into the bondage of reserves was not the ruin of a political and social system, but rather a healthy organism which had taken root and grown strong on the plains. The fate of the Plains Cree nation followed that of the buffalo—not to death, but into a white man's pound, the reserve."[2]

In the early 1870s the Plains Cree were still following annual cycles based on the changing seasons. In the spring these plains tribes still emerged from the protected shelter of the woodlands and river valleys onto the plains to gather in large numbers for the annual sun dance, where the men asked for power from the sun and invited visions that were induced by self-imposed fasting, and the young men passed from adolescence into the adult life of their band or tribe. Contacts with neighboring groups were renewed, and military and trade strategies and policies were discussed.

After spring break-up, the people caught fish by extending weirs across streams and rivers, and in summer they lived in relative abundance off the harvest from the buffalo. Roots, berries, seeds, fruits, wild honey, wild rice, and maple syrup were plentiful and could be collected during the late summer. The prairie turnip or white apple was also harvested. As autumn approached, the large tribal unit began to break up into smaller groups and moved to the protection of the parklands away from the Blackfoot and in search of a haven from severe winter weather. Some of the older men would go in search of large game such as moose and elk, and food was prepared to last through the winter months. Pemmican was made and stored. It was high in protein and could last for years. Often it was all that carried the Cree through the harsh winter months. Large stocks of pemmican, tallow, dried meat, and buffalo robes were set aside to trade to the HBC in the spring.

Winter was accompanied by hardship. Individual members of each band or family would stalk game in the snow. In the shelter of the tents, the myths and stories of these people were rekindled along with accounts of recent exploits, perhaps to become future legends. Crafts were also a common activity in winter, as were sports and games that included popular forms of gambling. Furs to be traded in spring were collected and prepared. After enduring the long winter nights, the Cree looked to the sky for signs of spring and rebirth as each year was lived out in response to the rhythms of nature. To them life unfolded in cycles and there was no sense of linear progression as each year passed.

The Christian world view brought to the plains by the European missionaries stood in stark contrast to that of the plains tribes. European Christians did not live in proximity to nature and did not seek communion with nature as the Indians did. Rather, they adopted an adversarial attitude toward nature and viewed it with suspicion and fear. Nature was something to be conquered or overcome, as were their own emotional and physical desires. The Christian world view was human-centered and only incidentally concerned itself with seasonal cycles. The Christian god was one to be feared. According to some religious dogma, humans to appease this god would need to toil on earth and prove their worth to avoid damnation and burning for eternity in hell, a concept alien to Indian religion. In Indian beliefs, an individual might be denied the fruits of a pursuit because a spirit power had not been properly appeased, but the consequence was not the eternal damnation of the Christian god.

Through their fur-trade contacts, Indians were familiar with Christian concepts. The European traders had not, however, made any attempts to convert them. As missionaries began arriving, it was soon apparent they were intent on converting to Christianity what they saw as a heathen, savage people. These Christian missionaries, unlike Indian religious men or shamans, had what has been described as a compulsive need to convert Indians to Christianity. The missionaries felt threatened by an unknown they could not control.[3]

The biblical injunctions that informed and directed the missionaries compelled them to reject Indian culture and society. At the cornerstone stood the dictum from Genesis 1:2: "Be fruitful and multiply, and replenish the earth and subdue it: and have dominion over the fish of the sea; and over the fowl of the air, and over everything that moveth upon the earth." This was the directive for the Christian "sodbuster"—to "break" the soil and tame the land. By the mid-nineteenth century, Victorian Canadians had a boundless faith in their society and culture. They were proud of their railways, steamships, and factories; they were confident that during their lifetimes, man was reaching the pinnacle of his mission to subdue the earth.

The band and tribal life of most plains people stood in stark contrast to the more aggressive dynamic that motivated Victorians of young industrial Canada. They did not have the same concept of structured society as Victorian Canadians. Though they had often adjusted to changing circumstances, plains tribes still followed the seasonal cycles and pulse of nature and not the Newtonian clock of absolute time ticking by the second. These contrasting concepts of time made it easy for the Europeans to criticize what appeared to them as laziness, since their unit for measuring the time by which tasks were to be accomplished, the second, was much smaller than the units familiar to Indians. The Europeans seemed to race against time to harvest what they saw as the vast potential for power around them.

There were other characteristics of tribal society that made Victorian Canadians critical of the Indian way of life. Their apparently casual attitude toward private property was quite alien to Europeans, who felt accumulation of wealth by the individual was an important way to evaluate each person's value. The movement of people across the plains without an easily perceptible purpose was seen as evidence of a shiftless people, ill-equipped by religion and unprepared by culture to recognize the value of property ownership. Private property was seen by Victorians as a prerequisite in establishing a work ethic and the desire to strive for improvement. Hunting was not a respected pursuit to the Victorian frame of mind unless as a sport or pastime. A lifestyle based on a feast or famine cycle was thought to be "improvident" and evidence that Indians, whose economy was based on hunting, were incapable of careful planning for the future. To live so close to nature and to be virtually at its mercy was an indication of a "primitive" society; not to accumulate a surplus proved a lack of mastery over nature. By the 1880s, as plains peoples became increasingly destitute and dependent on Whites, many Canadians believed they had been proved right. To them, the Indians' inability to make the land fruitful by settling and their preference of wandering in pursuit of game was evidence of a people that did not live correctly. Indeed their own way of life seemed to flourish next to that of the Indians.

It was the European concept of private property that was eventually to destroy Indian claims to use of the western prairie, and it was the consequences of implementing this idea that ultimately would erode their way of life. The concept of property title for land ownership was alien to the Indian peoples, yet in a short time what seemed impossible was soon realized.

Attitudes toward "land use" changed on the prairies during the 1870s and 1880s. The transition (some would say the progression) went from land enjoyed in common, that is, to be used by all; to open access where land is claimed but can still be used by others; to entrenchment of land held legally as private property. Prior to the systematic settlement of the prairies, Indian society functioned on and perhaps survived through communal cooperation. They did not believe that anyone had sole rights to the resources: "Game was the common property of all, and everyone had a chance to share in this gift of nature."[4] When passing through territory held by Indians, individuals were free to take or use any resources needed, whether that be game, water, or fuel.

The plains tribes were "a people who had no notion of exclusive and permanent property rights in land or the other gifts of the Great Spirit."[5] Those with a wealth of resources in band or tribal society would share with those less fortunate; it was considered a matter of pride and an indication of status to be able to give to those who were in need. These people were in fact living amid wealth and by the nature of their culture did not need to be conspicuous consumers. Their environment was rich with resources: wood, water, forage, game, fish, berries, honey, wild rice, clothing, housing, weapons, implements, toys, and thread. To have access to all this, however, a great freedom of movement was required. Farming, which meant a more sedentary life, was only incidental to plains life, and agricultural products were usually obtained by trade. Plains Indians thus moved with the seasons, following the migrations and cycles of wildlife.

Most obviously disruptive to this lifestyle was the disappearance of the buffalo herds, which led the Indians to a greater dependence on other food sources and increased agriculture. Their movements were not only restricted by this development but also by the increasing settlement of the plains. At first, through the 1870s, those Indians who had not yet signed a treaty protested against White settlers and interlopers who simply occupied territory and gave nothing back in return. It is not clear if they understood the settlers were actually claiming the land. "Emphasis was on the use of lands—indeed, it seems probable that the Indian thought of the problem as that of the right to use their lands . . . the outright sale of those lands was a concept entirely unfamiliar to them."[6] Gradually more of their resources such as fish, wood for fuel, and game were not only being depleted but exploited.

European discourses concerning Indians were damaging and unsympathetic, especially when describing the culture and society of plains people. Europeans had equated living in harmony with nature as "savage" and exploiting nature as "civilized." But Indian land use and movement with the seasons were in fact evidence of a dynamic, adaptable way of life, quite in contrast to the images of a largely moribund and static people that Europeans presented:

> Native economies in America were not poorer, more precarious, or more miserable than their contemporary European counterparts. Indeed, recent studies of hunting and gathering societies suggest that natives of the western interior may have lived a life of relative comfort and plenty.[7]

THE DOWNSTREAM PEOPLE AND TREATY 4

The Aboriginal people who commonly used the Cypress Hills area at the time the NWMP arrived in the West were mostly the Downstream people who eventually took reserves in the Qu'Appelle Valley. The Downstream people of the Touchwood Hills, File Hills, and Qu'Appelle Valley were distinguished from the Cree north of the South Saskatchewan River or the Upstream people. These people were Saulteaux, Assiniboin, and Plains Cree. A western group of these Downstream people—the Calling River People—were regularly found in the Cypress Hills in the 1870s. They often wintered in the Hills near Old Wives Lake and Swiftcurrent Creek.

One of the main chiefs of the Downstream people, the one recognized as the head chief of the Touchwood People, was Cawacatoose or Poor Man or Lean Man. He was noted as a brave warrior and it was said that he had gone to battle armed only with a lance made of a shoot of a saskatoon bush and topped with an iron head. His band participated in the famous battle of the Belly River in 1871 in which twenty of his people died. Other significant chiefs of the more easterly bands were Kaneonuskatew, He Who Walks on Four Claws or Gordon, as well as Kisecawchuck or Day Star. Day Star's band were known particularly for repelling an attack of the Blackfoot at Red Ochre Hill near Swift Current. Three hundred Blackfoot died, while only fifteen Cree fell. Other well-known chiefs included Kakeesheway or Loud Voice, who was acknowledged as the head chief by the HBC. He was highly regarded as a medicine man and as a military strategist.

Of the more western bands were the people of Kahkewistahaw or He Who Flies Around. This band hunted in an area that included the Cypress Hills. Kahkewistahaw was a distinguished scout, hunter, warrior, and linguist. He was a chief not highly regarded by the HBC and therefore was not likely heavily dependent on the fur trade. Another band that hunted in the Cypress Hills area was that of Chief Cowesses or Little Child. Among his members was the distinguished Saulteaux spokesman Louis O'Soup. Other chiefs who occupied this more westerly territory included Pasquah, whose band was predominantly Saulteaux.

Chief Piapot's Young Dogs or Little Dogs, a large band of Cree-Assiniboin people, also lived off land west and south of the Qu'Appelle country. Piapot was thought to have important contacts with the more southerly Assiniboin. Piapot's band in particular hunted in the Cypress Hills area, and also to the south as far as the Missouri River and north up to the South Saskatchewan River. As the buffalo disappeared, this group ventured farthest west in search of the diminishing herds. Piapot's band wintered in the Wood Mountain area and frequently in the eastern Cypress Hills as well. He was thought of as an honorable chief by the HBC but was also viewed as ambitious and troublesome. Again he was likely a chief more independent of the fur trade than some of the more easterly Down-stream people. Others among the chiefs who moved throughout this territory were White Calf, Peepeekis or Little Black Hawk, and Little Black Bear. The latter was a noted warrior and Cree leader at the battle of Red Ochre Hill.

These were the groups that were to sign Treaty 4. By the end of the 1870s the food crisis led missionaries in the area to refer to the situation among these people as appalling. The disappearing and receding buffalo herds had already led many of these Indians to supplement hunting with agriculture even before the signing of Treaty 4. Many people of these bands were already familiar with agriculture and were knowledgeable about their environment: the extent of the growing season, rainfall and frost patterns, soil varieties, availability of water, pasturage, and the local vegetation. They were well acquainted with the care of domesticated animals through their experience with their horses. By treaty time, however, starvation had reached such proportions that it was clear to these people that they would require some government assistance in order to make the transition to an economy based on agriculture.

In the pre-treaty years there were many suggestions from Ottawa by civil servants as to how to solve the problem of starvation and settlement of the Aboriginal people. Most of the suggestions were made by bureaucrats who had never been to the West and most of whom knew nothing about Native people. Their suggestions ranged from turning Indians into a pastoral people who would tend horses and cattle, to having them work on railroad crews and working as guides or constables for both the police and the military. Lessons had been learned from earlier treaties and John Christian Schultz, for one, argued that more money had to be spent by the government to ensure a proper transition to the agricultural way of life advocated for Indians. Schultz criticized the "paltry" annuity payment given in Treaties 1 and 2 and suggested more land be given—64 hectares (160 acres) instead of 16 hectares (40 acres) as stipulated in previous treaties. Schultz also recommended a sum of money be set aside from the land sales so that the people could be given an education.

In spite of the many grand suggestions, "the government disregarded the advice not only of Schultz but also of those who advocated the unique needs and characteristics of the people of the North-West to be taken into consideration in devising policy."[8] The government, instead of reconsidering existing policy, took the path of least resistance and simply adopted for the West the same approach they had taken to the treaties in the East. Large tracts of land were to be transferred to the Crown in advance of colonization. In return for relinquishment of title, the Aboriginal people were to receive annuities, reserves, and guarantees that they could continue to hunt on portions of the land they had given up to the Crown.

Amid fears that settlers would begin arriving before land issues were settled and amid apprehension about the presence of the telegraph, railing, and survey crews, the tribes began to pressure the government about its intentions for dealing with Aboriginal people. In 1874 Chief Poor Man sent his brother Kanocees to speak with Alexander Morris, lieutenant-governor of the North-West Territories, about the necessity of settling many issues that concerned the Indians. Thus the plains peoples took an active role in negotiating with the government. They were determined to have their voice heard: "By interfering with the survey, and preventing the construction of the telegraph, the Plains Indians made it clear that they would not allow settlement until their rights were fully recognized."[9] The other major concern of the Cree, Assiniboin, and Saulteaux leadership was that they be able to develop a new base of economic security for the future. This is clear from the speeches made by chiefs during the negotiations. Sweet Grass, an eloquent spokesman, stated the Indian position to Morris most felicitously:

> We heard our lands were sold and we did not like it; we don't want to sell our lands; it is our property, and no one has a right to sell them. Our country is getting ruined of fur-bearing animals, hither to our sole support, and now we are poor and want help—we want you to pity us. We want cattle, tools, agricultural implements, and assistance in everything when we come to settle—our country is no longer able to support us.[10]

Even though the government claimed its bargaining position was fixed and that it did not have the ability to alter terms of specific treaties, Indian negotiators were able to pressure Morris to agree to a number items of great concern to the Downstream people. Initially the government had offered only reserves and annuities, but the Indian negotiators demanded and secured the promise of implements and farm animals.

The negotiations that marked the Qu'Appelle treaty (Treaty 4) took place in September 1874. The government representatives consisted of Lt. Gov. Alexander Morris; David Laird, minister of the interior; and W. J. Christie, retired chief factor of the HBC. The Qu'Appelle people chose Loud Voice as their main spokesman. Among the three main groups—the Cree, the Assiniboin, and the Saulteaux—it was the latter who bargained the most vigorously. The Gambler, a Saulteaux chief, demanded that the issue of the HBC and their land be dealt with before any other items were settled.

They claimed that the three million pounds paid by Canada to the company should rightfully be theirs. They did not want the company trading in their territory, except at the posts, and they asked that the debts owed by the Indians to the company be cleared as some compensation for the company's profits from the transfer of their land.[11]

It was not until six days of negotiations passed that agreement was reached, and this without the influential bands of Piapot and Okanese present. Agriculture was thus to be the basis of new reserve economies:

To any band thereof who are now actually cultivating the soil, or who shall hereafter settle on these reserves and commence to break up the land, that in the say—two hoes, one spade, one scythe, and one axe for every family so actually cultivating; and enough seed, wheat, barley, oats, and potatoes to plant such lands as they have broken up; also one plough and two harrows for every ten families so cultivating as alone said; and also to each Chief, for the use of his band as aforesaid, one yoke of oxen, one bull, four cows, a chest of ordinary carpenter's tools, five hand-saws, five augers, one cross-cut saw, the necessary files, and one grindstone.[12]

By the time Treaty 6 was signed two years later, even more assistance for reserve agriculture was contained in the agreement. Treaty 6 signatories bargained for more spades and hoes, more ploughs and harrows per family, more livestock, a handmill, and an incentive of $1,000 paid each band that was cultivating the land after three years of signing the treaty. The additional assistance demanded by Treaty 6 Indians was a clear indication of their determination to see agriculture become a successful basis for a new economy, but it was also as a result of witnessing the difficulties Treaty 4 Indians were having: "They were aware of the limited progress made by the Treaty Four Indians, who did not have such provisions."[13]

SITTING BULL AND THE DAKOTA

The numbered treaties of 1871–76 had dealt with removing the threat of Indian uprisings, at least in the minds of government officials. Métis discontent, however, continued to fester since their land claims remained unsettled. In the meantime, an unexpected and potentially disastrous problem for Canadian authority in the Northwest was the appearance of the

Dakota (Teton or Lakota Sioux) in Canadian territory after they had destroyed an American military force commanded by Lt. Col. George A. Custer at the Little Big Horn. Generally, the American method of dealing with Indian populations south of the border differed dramatically from the Canadian approach. What Canadians hoped to achieve subtly, the Americans chose to achieve with force. In 1876 the Americans spent twenty million dollars fighting "Indian Wars," wars that literally cleared the land for White occupation. Canada could not afford such a solution—force was not only an expensive option, it was an impossible one. The numbered treaties, negotiation, and dialogue were the Canadian responses to the Aboriginal populations. The Mounted Police were the Canadian sign of authority, not the blue-coated cavalry that the Americans sent out to hunt down the Indians.

In conflicts at the edge of expanding empires a frontier altercation, however small, is an excuse for large-scale reprisals. This usually happens with the first pioneers of settlement or proselytizing missionaries who are mistreated or worse by local Aboriginal populations. In the specific American example that brought the Dakota to Canada it was neither God nor Glory that produced a fearful military response, but Gold.

The disputed territory that eventually led to the battle of the Little Big Horn was the Black Hills, now in South Dakota. The Dakota had always been a powerful tribe made up of many subgroups. The plains people of the Dakota had always moved about the American plains and even up into Canadian territory as the strength or weakness of groups on their fringes allowed. The Dakota also had historical connections with Canada dating back to the War of 1812, when the Dakota sided with the British to fight American forces in the West in a war that was crucial in preserving British, and eventually Canadian, territories from being annexed by the United States. The Dakota thus felt they had a right to Canada's protection in their own time of need.

Sitting Bull (Tatanka-Tyotanka), the spiritual leader of the Dakota, earned his name as the result of a fight while he was still a youth. In tribute, his father gave him his name, "Sitting Bull," and took for himself the name "Jumping Bull." In 1857, at the young age of twenty-six, he had become one of the war chiefs of the Hunkpapas and one of most influential leaders among the various Dakota tribes.[14] In spite of the legends about his military prowess, however, Sitting Bull was more renowned as a medicine man or political leader among his people than as a warrior.

With the Dakota in 1876 during their conflict with the American government were a group of Nez Percé Indians—so-called for their pierced noses. The Nez Percé had already come into conflict with White settlers in the mid-nineteenth century when settlers began to invade their territories throughout Oregon, Washington, and Idaho. A treaty had been signed with the Nez Percé; however, it took four years to ratify the treaty, which was to protect territories in these regions for use of the Indians. Gold discovered in 1861 brought hundreds of prospectors onto Nez Percé lands. The government ignored the 1855 agreement and replaced it in 1861 with an agreement that gave mining privileges to the gold diggers. A new treaty was drafted by the government in 1863 taking away seven-eighths of the land originally granted to the Nez Percé peoples. The Nez Percé chiefs, Joseph, Looking Glass, and White Bird, refused to sign the new treaty. The legacy of lies and betrayals that the Nez Percé had endured would also be the fate of the Dakota farther to the east.

The Indian Treaty of 1851 with the Dakota had protected their territories in the Big Horn Mountains from intrusion. The Dakota repeatedly asked that the Bozeman Trail run to the west so as to leave their hunting grounds unmolested. When the requests for negotiation went unheeded, a series of massacres and battles ensued throughout the territory. Among the most famous of these battles was one that took place in 1866 in which the Dakota were led by Chiefs Red Cloud and Man-Afraid-of-His-Horses. Whites already suspected that gold might be found in the hills occupied by the Cheyenne and Dakota, and the voracious greed already exhibited by gold seekers would undoubtedly mean excursions into these areas.

The Dakota had sworn among themselves that no one would reveal the presence of the gold they knew to be in the Black Hills. Eventually, after much bloodshed and acrimony, the United States Government and the Dakota sat down to negotiate the Laramie Treaty of 1868. In this treaty the U.S. government agreed to set aside lands and hunting grounds onto which no White could trespass without permission. Territories north of the Platte rivers and east of the Big Horn Mountains were designated as "Indian Territory." The forts in Dakota and Cheyenne territory were to be abandoned. Despite this treaty, the military presence in the territories continued, as did hostilities against the Indians. George Custer became famous for being an Indian fighter when he led the attack on the camp of peace chief Black Kettle in the Washita Valley in 1868. Many military leaders throughout the West adopted a confrontational attitude toward the Aboriginal peoples of newly created territories and declared open season on any Indian people found outside designated lands. It became clear that they intended no peaceful resolution to disputes over mining territory set aside for Indians.

The negotiated truce in the end mattered little, and Whites continued to trespass onto Indian lands. The military were unable to stop these incursions and often sided with the White settlers and gold miners. The Dakota were being antagonized and provoked to act against the many violations of the treaty. As a result of the constant breaches of the agreement, the United States Government sent Custer into the Black Hills to choose sites on which to establish forts—ostensibly to keep the peace. When Custer returned from his mission, he reported the presence of large gold deposits in the Hills. The result was predictable, and gold-crazed prospectors streamed into the Black Hills. As one U.S. military official wrote: "There never was a wilder grab for gold than the succeeding dash into the Black Hills in the face of solemn treaties."[15]

With the discovery of gold, the U.S. government attempted to keep the Dakota out of the Hills, but they refused. In response to the resulting chaos and the violation of the treaty, Sitting Bull called for armed resistance and, along with Crazy Horse of the Oglala and Gall and Rain-in-the-Face of the Hunkpapas, he began to gather his people along the Powder River.

As discouraged and starving Dakota began to join the ranks of Sitting Bull and Crazy Horse, the U.S. government issued an ultimatum declaring that any Indians who did not return to their allocated reservations by January 31, 1876, would be regarded as enemies of the state and force would be used to return them there. The order had been issued on December 6, 1875, and compliance was impossible.

The army was ordered to proceed against those in violation of the ultimatum. When spring arrived after the extremely difficult winter of 1875–76, the Dakota now faced an army eager to contain and then defeat them. The command of the American forces was given to Brig. Gen. Alfred H. Terry with support from Col. John Gibbon, Gen. George Crook, as well as the 7th Cavalry of Lt. Col. George Custer. There was to be no quarter given, the campaign against the Dakota and Cheyenne was to be complete and decisive: the people would return to the reservations or the military would force them there. The U.S. armies moved against the Native people from the north, east, and south. Early in the confrontation Crook attacked a large camp of Dakota and Cheyenne at Rosebud Creek, but was unable to defeat them. The presence of large and determined American military forces led some chiefs, such as Red Cloud, to return to their reservations, but not the determined Sitting Bull and his followers.

The strategy of Terry was to locate and approach Sitting Bull's men and to attack only when every avenue for escape had been blocked. Converging armies were sent into the Big Horn Mountains. The commands of Gibbon and Custer were to meet in the Big Horn Valley on June 26. They were still unaware of the setback Crook had suffered at the hands of Crazy Horse on June 17.

The land between the Rosebud and Powder rivers was searched to locate the large concentration of people under Sitting Bull's leadership. On June 24, Custer, with the help of a Crow scout, found the Dakota moving across the Wolf Mountain divide. Custer's Crow scouts warned him that the large camp they located was too big to be engaged. Ignoring this wise advice, Custer gave orders to advance, intending to attack the Dakota before they could escape. He divided his twelve troops, amounting to six hundred men, into three columns in preparation for the attack. Custer did not consider waiting for Terry's or Gibbon's forces. The fighters with Sitting Bull numbered 2,500 to 3,000.

The middle column—Maj. Marcus A. Reno with three troops—was to move down a creek toward the Little Big Horn, and after moving down the valley, attack the village from the south. Capt. Frederick W. Benteen's three troops were to move to the left or south for a scout up the valley and then report back to the main body. Capt. Thomas M. McDougall, with one troop, brought up the rear and escorted the pack train. Custer and five troops moved parallel to Reno on the right to strike at the lower end of the village.

The planned coordinated attack of the columns failed and Custer, who had advanced far ahead of the others, was surrounded and killed with 215 of his men. The Crow scout Curly was the last survivor to see Custer alive.[16] The victors then attacked Reno and Benteen, but when the day ended the leaders of the Dakota and Cheyenne realized that there would be little point in prolonging the fighting. The consequences of an Indian force defeating a whole American army would be horrendous, and the Dakota leadership knew as much. The Dakota/Cheyenne alliance dispersed, with people moving off in different directions to avoid any pursuers. One group led by Crazy Horse moved southeast, hunted by Crook. The American military soon amassed an army of four thousand men to continue the campaign against the Dakota.

Sitting Bull had moved north toward Canada for safety. With some one thousand people he struck fear into the commanders of the northern forts, including Peck, Belknap, and Benton. Throughout the summer and into the fall the Dakota evaded the U.S. armies and hunted buffalo along the Milk River. Superintendent Walsh, who was on sick leave in the early summer, returned to Fort Walsh in the fall of 1876 and together with his scout Louis Léveillé tried to ascertain the whereabouts of the Dakota with Sitting Bull. So far no refugees had been found in Canadian territory but Walsh continued to send out patrols to locate the Dakota.

In November Sub-Inspector Edmond Frechette encountered the Dakota near Wood Mountain heading for Jean-Louis Légaré's trading post there. About half of Sitting Bull's Dakota were there and the remainder trailed not far behind, although the chief himself remained in Montana. When Walsh arrived in Wood Mountain in December there were an estimated 500 men, 1,000 women, and 1,400 children camped there. Close to the refugee camp was the settlement of White Eagle's Sisseton Dakota, who had fled to Canada following the 1862 rising of the Sioux known as the Minnesota Massacres.

White Eagle was of great assistance to Walsh and the NWMP. He was able to explain to the Dakota just arrived how the police operated and that they could expect fairness if they complied with Canadian law. The Dakota, through their great chief Black Moon, in return told Walsh that they were tired of being hunted, that they wanted nothing more than to rest peacefully in Canadian territory, and that they had no intention of launching an attack on the American forts in the northern states. The Dakota then begged Walsh for some ammunition in order to hunt, as their long trek north had left them in a state of starvation. Walsh cautioned them against using the ammunition for any other purpose and made it clear that it could not be sent across the border to aid those still actively resisting the authorities. The Dakota reassured Walsh that such was not their intention, and Walsh allowed Légaré, the local trader, to distribute the ammunition—to the great relief and gratitude of the hungry Dakota.

The arrival of the Dakota onto Canadian soil produced a series of problems that the Mounties had to be aware of and be ready to handle. First, the Dakota were traditional enemies of the Plains Cree and Saulteaux peoples, as well as of the Blackfoot. This could lead to strained relations and conflict, especially if they came into competition for the same food supplies. Luckily in the winter of 1876 there were plenty of buffalo in the Wood Mountain area and shortages were not likely to arise in the short term, but a longer stay might change these circumstances. Also, there was the potential for problems resulting from border incidents that might bring American armies into conflict not only with the Dakota but with other Canadian Indian peoples as well.

Walsh had come out to meet the first group of several thousand Dakota with but twelve men. Thus astute negotiations and trust were what the police had most to rely on. The Mounties had to rely on the weight of their moral authority, since they were not likely to be able to settle very much through a show of force. American military authorities greatly feared further attacks from the Dakota, so the NWMP had not only to pacify and control the Dakota in their territory, but they also had to reassure the American generals (some of them anxious for reprisals) not to worry about the refugees on Canadian soil. A further issue that concerned the Mounties was whether Sitting Bull would be able to unite otherwise disparate tribal peoples into an alliance to fight the Americans and recover the buffalo hunting territory that they at one time dominated.

There were other possibilities that the Mounties had to be aware of. One of these was the potential for an alliance between Louis Riel, now living in Montana, with the disaffected Indians gathered around Sitting Bull. All of these issues meant the NWMP had to act carefully and judiciously both in gathering information and in interpreting the intelligence gathered. The situation throughout the Northwest became tense as buffalo migrations onto the Canadian prairies became less and less frequent. Many peoples such as the Peigan, Blood, Sarsi, Blackfoot, Saulteaux, Assiniboin, Cree, Gros Ventre, Crow, and Métis relied on this staple for survival.

In order to handle the dangerous situation, Walsh increased the police presence at subposts east of the main fort on the Cypress Hills. This increased the ability of the police to keep up a proper surveillance of the Dakota refugees and helped in maintaining the communications necessary for a successful negotiated settlement of the crisis. One of these outposts was at the eastern end of the Cypress Hills, appropriately named East End, approximately 72 kilometers (45 mi) from the main fort, and the other was at Wood Mountain, 208 kilometers (130 mi) away. In addition, to assist with gathering information and for proper communication, Joseph Morin, a Métis interpreter, was hired by the Mounties and stationed at Wood Mountain.

Skirmishes between the Dakota and the American armies in pursuit of them continued throughout the fall. There were several confrontations between the Dakota and the U.S. forces that included the people with Sitting Bull. Also at large were Crazy Horse and his followers, who never ventured into Canada but whose whereabouts were of great concern until their surrender on May 6, 1877, at Red Cloud Agency. Gradually, as starvation continued and pressure by the U.S. military continued, the ranks of the Dakota resisting relocation were thinned.

In the spring of 1877, three thousand Dakota people gave themselves up at the Red Cloud, Spotted Tail, and Cheyenne River agencies and returned to their reservations. Three hundred Cheyenne also surrendered at the Tongue River Cantonment. A calm descended around the Wood Mountain area in the winter of 1876–77. The Dakota brought furs and skins to

Légaré's trading post and virtually cleaned him out of his supplies of tea, tobacco, sugar, flour, as well as beads and decorative items. Légaré remained cautious about the presence of the Dakota, however. For Walsh, winter conditions made travel difficult: it took nine days to travel from Wood Mountain to Fort Walsh—a trip that took half that time in the summer or fall.

Early in 1877 surveillance of the border lands continued as rumors of more Dakota moving north were investigated. Walsh himself took a central role in this activity. Together with the Métis scouts Morin, Léveillé, and Daniels he kept up a constant survey of the "Bad Lands" that surrounded the valley of the Whitemud River. Walsh found it necessary to intercept Indians coming into Canadian territory in order to explain to them what to expect over the border. Such an occasion occurred when he approached a camp of Dakota following Four Horns, who was in search of Sitting Bull's camp. Suspicion clouded many of the initial encounters between the NWMP and the Dakota. The Indians feared that the "Red Coats" might be acting in support of the "Long Knives," and it often took considerable persuasion before such fears were alleviated. In the first encounter with Four Horns it was eventually the reputation of Walsh as a fair-minded policeman that won the trust of the refugees.

In April 1877, after the arrival of Four Horns, rumors spread that Sitting Bull was approaching the border. With a handful of Mounties and scouts Louis Léveillé and Gabriel Solomon, Walsh again swept the area to intercept the refugees before they reached the main body of the Dakota camp. On May 1, the first meeting between Sitting Bull and Walsh, Sitting Bull made it clear that he did not want to fight with Canadian authorities, that he had laid down his arms at the border, and that he had only been fighting previously because he had to. Walsh told Sitting Bull, as he had told the other chiefs Black Moon, Four Horns, and Medicine Bear, that they would be supplied with sufficient ammunition to hunt for food and that in return the Dakota were subject to the Queen's law and that no breach would be tolerated. In the language of the day, they were told they could "sleep without fear." In a long exchange of speeches Walsh was told by Chief Spotted Eagle that the Dakota in his group finally crossed the border because they feared for the lives of their women and children.

Walsh stayed in the Dakota camp the evening after the first meeting. In the morning, as he was preparing to leave, three men came riding into the Dakota camp with some horses. Among them was an Assiniboin known as White Dog, who was recognized by Gabriel Solomon as a horse thief. Among the horses brought into the camp were a number that had been stolen the previous year in the Cypress Hills. Walsh, determined to make the arrest, walked into a large group of Dakota soldiers where White Dog had sought safety and moved to arrest him. After Walsh demanded an explanation from White Dog, which he accepted, the Assiniboin was freed (he said the horses were found astray). The horses were kept by the police to be returned to owners in the Cypress Hills. The incident was an indication to the Dakota of how the Mounties acted in most cases: fair and firm.

The presence of the Dakota in the traditional hunting territory of the Assiniboin and Saulteaux produced tensions not only with the Dakota but between these other tribes as well. In May of 1877, a large group of American Assiniboin led by Crow's Dance had attempted to intimidate a group of Canadian Saulteaux to join their numbers. The Saulteaux under Little Child complained to Walsh about the incident and he set off to the Assiniboin camp, again outnumbered. Walsh arrested Crow's Dance, Crooked Arm, and eleven other Assiniboin. After a series of trials, Crow's Dance was given a six-month sentence, Crooked Arm two, and the eleven others were released. It was again an indication to all in the Northwest that the law was going to be enforced.

In their first encounters with the police, the Dakota who arrived in Canada were eager to show their ties to the Crown. They related in their speeches how their history had given them a special tie to Canada. They had fought with the British in 1812 and for this reason they expected to be given sanctuary in the lands of their British allies. They expected to be protected in the land of the Great White Mother.

The Canadian government, for its part, had no intention of allowing its once-loyal allies to remain in Canada. In the summer of 1877, Assistant Commissioner Irvine went to meet with Sitting Bull to discuss the situation. An American emissary, Father Martin Marty, head of the Roman Catholic Diocese of Dakota Territory, had come to the Dakota camp to persuade the Dakota to return to American territory, but Sitting Bull refused, having assurances—for the time being at least—that he would be protected on Canadian soil. Father Marty and the two other Americans with him were lucky to have gotten out of Sitting Bull's camp with their lives. Their efforts failed enormously and it would now fall on the shoulders of Canadian authorities to dissuade the Dakota from staying in Canada. It was clear the Long Knives and their representatives were thoroughly hated by the Dakota.

The commissioner of the NWMP, James F. Macleod, urgently advised Ottawa that the Dakota could not be allowed to remain on Canadian soil as they were viewed with suspicion by both the Blackfoot and the Cree. The truce on the Canadian prairie between the various Native peoples was uneasy at best, and the Washington and London diplomatic services should be advised of the problem at once. This advice was sent to the official diplomatic services even though the police in fact expected no trouble from the Dakota. The Mounties respected the Dakota leadership and believed the expression of peaceful intention by the chiefs. The Dakota, on the other hand, had shown great interest in remaining in Canada with the same right accorded those Dakota who came to stay in Canada after the Minnesota Massacres of 1862. But no one wanted the Dakota in the Wood Mountain area: neither the Blackfoot, nor the Cree, nor the Assiniboin, nor the Métis; neither the Mounties, nor the United States Government, nor the Canadian government.

American Indian policy complicated matters even further when the Nez Percé were given an ultimatum to move to their reservation voluntarily or be driven there by force. They were given thirty days from early May to comply with the order. The Nez Percé asked for more time but this was denied them. With the same defiance exhibited by the Dakota, the Nez Percé refused to move to the new reservation and the younger men among them organized a war party. Others decided to leave the country. By June 13, the time given by the authorities to take the new reservation had run out and war was on. The Nez Percé won some early successes against the U.S. military forces but by September, outnumbered and with little left to fight with, they began to move northward from the battle grounds of the Musselshell River toward the Bear's Paw Mountains. This put them within a day's journey of the Canadian border and the same safety enjoyed by the Dakota with Sitting Bull. General Miles in pursuit of the Nez Percé had located them in the Bear's Paw Mountains but had been unable to defeat them. What he feared most was an attack from the Dakota in Canada, since he had suffered heavy losses against the Nez Percé soldiers.

By October, Chief Joseph recognized the futility of continued resistance and gave up. However, the requests he had made for assistance from Sitting Bull's forces had wrought havoc for Walsh and his Mountie scouts throughout the territory between Wood Mountain and the Bear's Paw Mountains. There was a constant stream of messengers to and from Sitting Bull's councilors, and the young men of the Dakota were eager to go and deliver a final defeat to the hated American forces. Walsh spent much time among the Dakota warning them that if they crossed the border to fight the Americans they would become the enemy of Canadian authorities as well. In the end, only White Bird, with a group of 98 Nez Percé men and about twenty women and children, escaped the siege imposed by Miles's troops in the Bear's Paw Mountains.

On October 8, rumors circulated that the Americans were proceeding north to attack the Dakota (having just defeated the Nez Percé). The fears were unfounded; instead the police and the Dakota discovered the straggling band of unfortunate and desperate Nez Percé under White Bird. These refugees were given sanctuary away from their hated American pursuers and were taken into the care of the Dakota. The Nez Percé who had surrendered to the Americans numbered only about 200 to 250. Those captured were to be taken to reservations set aside in Oklahoma, many hundreds of kilometers (miles) from their homelands in Oregon.

Another mission by a cleric, Father Jean Baptiste Genin, was undertaken in October 1877 to persuade the Dakota to return to American territory. Father Genin's mission, like previous attempts at persuasion, failed. Genin, however, expressed the criticism that the Dakota would not budge because they were being too well treated by the NWMP and that their stay in Canada was becoming too comfortable for them.

Finally it was up to an official American delegation to attempt to negotiate the return of the Dakota. The Terry Commission had been established and was to proceed to Canadian territory and assemble at Fort Walsh to persuade, not coerce, a return of the Dakota people. The American commissioners were met at the border and were escorted to Fort Walsh to begin their discussions, having telegraphed ahead in early September that they were on their way. NWMP Commissioner James F. Macleod, who had led the negotiation of Treaty 7 in Alberta, made his way to Fort Walsh, the proposed scene of the talks to be held with Sitting Bull. The officials with the NWMP were in a state of some disbelief that the Americans were sending General A. H. Terry to conduct the negotiations, since it had been Terry who in the previous year had been commander-in-chief of the military forces sent against the Dakota.

Walsh was assigned the task of approaching Sitting Bull about attending the talks at Fort Walsh. This was not an easy job. Terry was hated not only by the Dakota but by the Nez Percé as well. He had a reputation among them for having shot innocent women and children of both the Dakota and Nez Percé people. A. G. Lawrence, his co-commissioner, was also not well loved by the Dakota: in 1875 he was with the force that took the Black Hills from their possession.

Sitting Bull did not want to attend any talks with Terry. He had no reason to believe any of the inducements offered after seeing his own people so recently robbed of their own homes and lands—hunted down like animals when they did not obey the arbitrary dictates of American officials. When Walsh was unable to persuade Sitting Bull, he asked his scouts Louis Léveillé and Joseph "Blackbird" Morin to talk to Sitting Bull in Dakota. When this failed he asked two more Métis scouts, Antoine Ouilette and André Larivée, to speak to Sitting Bull. This final attempt at persuasion succeeded and Sitting Bull agreed to talk to the Americans under heavy escort.

Macleod had arrived at Fort Walsh on October 1. General Terry was to be at the border five days later. For the negotiations, Walsh traveled from east of Fort Walsh with approximately twenty Dakota representatives including, among others, Spotted Eagle, Bear's Cap, Flying Bird, Storm Bear, Iron Dog, The Crow, The-Man-that-Scatters-the-Bear, Little Knife, and Yellow Dog. Those in the delegation had already told Walsh they had no intention of surrendering to the Americans.

On October 15, in a grand ceremony at the border, Commissioner James F. Macleod met the American delegation. General Terry proceeded north to Fort Walsh, leaving three companies of cavalry behind at the border, but taking one company of infantry north as an escort. On the sixteenth, the cavalcade reached Fort Walsh. That evening Sitting Bull again told Walsh he had no intention of making any concessions to Terry and that he had been deceived so often by the Americans that he was not about to be tricked again. The position of the Americans was that the Dakota could return to the U.S. unmolested, but that this was only on condition that they give up their guns and horses and return to their reservations. In the negotiating team for the U.S. were Terry, Lawrence, and the stenographer, Mr. Jan Stone. The party also included Jerome B. Stillson of the *New York Herald* and Charles Diehl of the *Chicago Times*.[17]

On October 17, the opposing sides sat across two small tables in the Officer's Mess, the largest room in the fort. The Dakota representatives sat on buffalo robes on the floor, while the Americans sat at two small tables across from them. The room was crowded with reporters, NWMP representatives, interpreters, and observers. The U.S. negotiators admitted apprehension in securing the return of Sitting Bull's Dakota back to the American territory, saying they still feared the Dakota might continue hostilities against them, if given the chance.

Sitting Bull arrived at the negotiations mid-afternoon wearing a red band of mourning for a son who had recently died. The other major negotiators for the Dakota were Spotted Eagle and The-Man-that-Scatters-the-Bear. Sitting Bull began the ceremony by taking out a pipe and lighting it. They then shook hands and Sitting Bull requested that the tables in the room be removed as he said they blocked his view of the American negotiators. The tables were removed.

Terry spoke to the Dakota first saying that the commission had been established by the president to negotiate a lasting peace and an end to the hostilities. The Dakota were asked to agree to stop fighting and to return to their reservations. The government extended an immunity to the Dakota, and they were assured that no legal action would be taken against them for any of the previous fighting. Those who returned would be treated in the same way as those who had surrendered. Sitting Bull was assured that none of the Dakota who had surrendered and returned to the reservations had been punished, and that they had been given food and clothing. Cattle had also been purchased for the surrendering people. In return the government expected the Dakota to give up their weapons and ammunition. Any horses deemed to be extra or for possible use in war would have to be surrendered. As well the Dakota would have to return to their assigned reservations. Terry, perhaps the worst emissary that the government could have sent, was sneered at and mocked with gestures by the Dakota as he spoke. To the Dakota, the Americans could not be serious by sending a man responsible for so many deaths.

Sitting Bull rose dramatically and began by relating the history of the treaty process the Dakota had experienced with the U.S. government. He spoke of the broken promises and the persecution. He accused Terry of telling lies and the government of taking lands away from his people. He walked up to Commissioner Macleod and Superintendent Walsh, shaking their hands saying that he would stay in Canada. Sitting Bull's speech was a bitter denunciation of the Americans. Others spoke as well. The-One-that-Runs-the-Ree said simply to the commissioners: "We don't like you." Another rebuked the Americans saying, "You came here to tell lies." When Terry asked whether he was to report this refusal to return, Sitting Bull responded vigorously, telling him he did not belong in Canada, that it was not his land. Sitting Bull then left the building.

Macleod followed Sitting Bull to speak to him about the situation. Macleod told Sitting Bull that even though he claimed to be a British Indian, in the eyes of the Canadian authorities he was not. The government and the NWMP considered him to be an American. They would therefore receive none of the benefits offered to Canadian treaty Indians. Macleod warned Sitting Bull that the buffalo were increasingly scarce throughout the country and that when they were gone his people would be reduced to dire destitution. Sitting Bull responded to Macleod saying that they were British Indians and expressed his hatred of the Americans for stealing the lands of their ancestral home in the Black Hills:

> The Great Spirit gives us plenty of buffalo. . . . I know you will
> not let the Long Knives harm us. The Americans gave us sweet
> words; they promised us flour and cattle, but if we go back, they
> will kill us. . . . I could never live there again. . . . We did not
> wish to fight. They started it. . . . Here is nothing but good. If
> they liked me, as they say, why did they drive me away? Today
> you heard one of our women speak to the Americans—she
> spoke the truth. We want to raise our children and be friends
> with all people here. We will live in peace with the red children
> of the Great White Mother. . . . We are friends with you and the
> other officers; it was on that account that we came to meet the
> Americans today.[18]

Sitting Bull then assured Macleod that they had absolutely no intention of going back to the border with Terry. He assured Macleod that they would live peaceably in the land and would obey the laws. The next day, October 18, Terry and his delegation returned to the border. The Dakota visited the fort and a feast was held.

Walsh had told the Americans that in time both the Nez Percé and Dakota would be ready to return to the U.S. The Mounted Police were also successful in arranging for another negotiation that it was hoped would lead to the return of the Dakota. On July 1, 1878, Assistant Commissioner Irvine had arranged for the Nez Percé chiefs Yellow Bull and Bald Head to meet with representatives of the American authorities at Fort Walsh. After extended negotiations between Lt. George Baird of the 5th Infantry and the Nez Percé over the fate of Chief Joseph, the Nez Percé eventually decided to stay in Canada, but these negotiations had at least made a start and the position of each group was now better understood by their opposing numbers.

Tensions throughout 1878 were kept up with constant rumors that Riel was planning to organize a great alliance of prairie Native peoples including the Blackfoot, Dakota, Assiniboin, Cree, and Métis. Walsh spent a good deal of his time in the Wood Mountain region trying to assess the truth of these rumors. Further anxiety resulted from prairie fires that had been lit just south of the 49th parallel that burned off the grass so that the buffalo were unable to move into Canadian territory. This greatly distressed the already destitute plains people and produced numerous rumors as to who should be blamed for these fires. Some said it was Sitting Bull trying to make it appear the Americans were responsible and in so doing hoping to incite other tribes to join him against the Long Knives. Others said the ultimate aim of the U.S. army was to starve the Dakota into returning to their reserves. It appears that the fires were set neither by Sitting Bull nor by the U.S. military, but rather by hunters trying to keep the buffalo to the south for commercial reasons. The slaughter of the great herds for the buffalo-robe trade continued unabated.

The destitution caused by the diminishing resources led eventually to a weakening of the resolve of some of the Dakota on Canadian soil. In the winter of 1880, sixty lodges of Dakota under the leadership of Spotted Eagle headed for their reservation and then a further twenty lodges followed the initial group. The suffering was great for those who remained. Sitting Bull's camp was plagued with disease and starvation, often resulting in death. By the spring of 1879 the want was so great in the camp of Sitting Bull that the Mounties shared their rations and Légaré supplied the starving people with everything he had left in his store. In spite of these circumstances, Sitting Bull and about two hundred lodges in his following preferred to stay in Canada and hoped to settle there.

Walsh maintained that even the Dakota who remained with Sitting Bull might have returned to their agencies in the U.S. had troops under Gen. Nelson A. Miles, victor over the Nez Percé, not continued to harass both Métis and Indian hunters who ventured south of the border in search of food. Their move into U.S. territory was motivated by starvation alone and was not in any way undertaken to provoke hostilities.

In the summer of 1879 it was the level head of Walsh that once again calmed and blunted the aggressive intentions of U.S. forces under Miles. Miles had been sent to the border area because of reports of horse stealing and general lawlessness but instead found Métis and Indian hunters searching for the last of the buffalo. Walsh, who had come into U.S. territory because of reports of conflict, explained to the American cavalry that it was need alone that caused these people to move across the border. Miles and his forces were determined to drive out all "foreign" Métis and Indians. His troops opened fire on the hunting parties and killed a number of innocent victims.

Walsh was able to secure the release of a large number of Métis that had been taken into custody by Miles. He still had to deal with the Dakota, however, some of whom were anxious for revenge against the Americans for casualties to their hunters. Walsh had to warn them that they were no longer allowed to venture onto American territory, even if only to hunt. The Dakota were getting an unpleasant impression indeed of the authorities who were sending emissaries to Canada asking for the peaceable return of the Dakota to their reservations. The hand of peace was extended but the threat of the gun was close behind.

Thus the role of the Mounties to persuade the Dakota to return was made more difficult by the aggressive and ill-considered actions of the American military authorities. Sitting Bull's position remained firm, as he had come to despise the Americans. After the confrontation with Miles he was said to have uttered to Walsh: "So long as there remains a gopher to eat, I will not go back."[19] The visits by missionaries such as the Reverend Mr. Marty and others did more to prevent the return of the Dakota than if they had simply been left alone, as Walsh knew full well.

Despite the tremendous workload borne by Walsh and his sensitive handling of most difficult situations, he was assigned a new position at Qu'Appelle, away from Wood Mountain and its responsibilities with the Dakota. Walsh was appalled by Superintendent L. N. F. Crozier, who was never able to gain the respect of the Dakota. Ironically some officials had wanted Walsh removed from his command because he was doing too good a job in his dealings with the Dakota: "The friendship that developed between Walsh and Sitting Bull may have been the major reason for the lack of serious troubles involving the Sioux in western Canada. Walsh was, however, criticized for becoming too friendly with Sitting Bull and for failing to persuade him to return to the United States."[20] So wrote his official biographer to explain the rather strange handling of James Walsh by his superiors.

Whatever the motivation for Walsh's removal, the Dakota did ask Walsh, as a last request, to approach officials in Washington for reassurance that they would be treated fairly when and if they returned. Walsh promised to do so. The Dakota may in fact have felt less secure in Canada without their friend close at hand. By the end of 1880 Walsh assured the commissioner that the departure of Sitting Bull from Canada would happen shortly. He said that Sitting Bull's power had been eroded (especially by Walsh himself) as other chiefs had agreed to return and members of his own camp wanted to return.

The old tactic of divide and conquer had worked once again. Throughout the winter of 1880 small groups of Dakota returned to the U.S., including some of the most persistent, such as the young leader Low Dog. Walsh, no longer with authority in the region, wrote: "I am in hopes that in a few weeks our territory will be rid of these troublesome intruders; we will then breathe more freely, and I for one will with all my heart say good bye to the old warrior. . . . I assure you they will be a good riddance."[21]

By the end of the winter of 1880–81 there was even more desperation in the camp of Sitting Bull. They had virtually nothing to trade for food and they had no prospects. Crozier was now in command and had threatened the Dakota to leave on a number of occasions. Feasts were held to entice the starving Dakota to leave. Crozier and Légaré made promises of provisions, horses, guns, and ammunition if only they would leave. A small number left with Légaré in April but most of them stayed behind, living primarily off some of his supplies. By not providing the ammunition and assistance that were given to treaty Indians, the Canadian authorities were shamefully watching the Dakota make the only choice that now seemed left open to them.

By May, Légaré had persuaded another group of thirty destitute and pathetic followers of Sitting Bull to head for Fort Buford in Dakota Territory. By June, the Dakota had moved to Qu'Appelle in hopes of meeting with Walsh and were raising the fears of the population throughout that area. In the end the Dakota were enticed back to Wood Mountain by the promise of food. In early July, Sitting Bull made his last bargain for food and supplies from Légaré to tide his people over for the trip to Fort Buford. Flour, wagons, and ponies were given to the now almost totally destitute band left with Sitting Bull. They were met by the Americans at the border and assured of a safe passage. They reached Fort Buford, Dakota Territory, on July 19.

Légaré had delivered 235 Dakota to the fort. Only a handful of the original group remained around Wood Mountain when Légaré returned. Many, including Légaré, Walsh, and Crozier, as well as Commissioners Macleod and Irvine, had done their best to make the Dakota leave Canada. The incident remains a regrettable page in the history of Canada. The people that were one-time military allies to the British during their time of need were not granted asylum when this position was reversed.

Sitting Bull himself was proved right in his mistrust of the Americans, whom he believed were liars and despised so much. In 1890, at the instigation of Indian Agent James McLaughlin, he was shot by tribal police on the Standing Rock Reservation in South Dakota. Like Gabriel Dumont, Sitting Bull had toured briefly in Buffalo Bill's Wild West Show, entertaining American audiences in the years before his death. The final assessment of Sitting Bull by one biographer was that he was "the greatest Indian chief of his time, perhaps of all time, he was considered a hero by some and a savage murderer by others."[22]

The NWMP, of course, played no small role in the whole affair, and Canadians have congratulated themselves by focusing on the friendship developed between Walsh and Sitting Bull. It was a friendship that was betrayed. Like so many others in hierarchical organizations, Walsh could claim he was merely following orders. But Walsh seemed genuine, if not sentimental (to assuage his guilt), when he wrote in his final assessment of Sitting Bull: "He was not the bloodthirsty man reports from the prairies made him out to be. He asked for nothing but justice . . . he was not a cruel man, he was kind of heart; he was not dishonest, he was truthful."[23]

Following the diminished threat posed by Sitting Bull, the attention of the police in the Cypress Hills turned primarily to the control and surveillance of local Cree, Assiniboin, and Métis populations. The Parliamentary Sessional Papers of the time suggest that more than half the arrests made concerning liquor, property (especially cattle and horse theft), and assault were of Aboriginal peoples.[24] There was no doubt that these groups were the focus of the police's concerns. As the military role of patrolling the border became less significant, the need to enforce social standards and laws consistent with the hegemony of the Anglo-Canadian presence that the police represented became more concentrated. The police themselves saw their role as one of civilizing the territory. The suggested implication in their belief that they represented those who legitimately were bringing civilization to the West left no doubt about who they thought comprised the "savage" half of the civilization-savagery equation.

CHAPTER 7

THE MODERN AGE

Treaty 4, signed in 1874, included the Saulteaux, Cree, and Assiniboin Indians between Fort Ellice and the Cypress Hills. Treaty 4 produced some tough negotiations between Alexander Morris, who was then treaty commissioner, and Indian leaders The Gambler and Pasquah, who put at issue the land that the HBC had occupied. The Indians claimed that money for extinguishment of title from the Company should have gone to the Indians, who had never given up their title, and not to the Canadian government. Eventually, after tactics by the government of separating militant Indians from the more passive ones succeeded, most of the Indians signed the treaty agreements and moved onto reserves.

Many of the Indians who had congregated in the Cypress Hills settled on reserves at Crooked and Round lakes in the Qu'Appelle Valley during the early 1880s. This was described as "a most beautiful part of the country, right on the Northern [sic] edge of the great plains, [with] fine poplar bluffs, some small lakes and the choices of wheat land, an ideal location chosen by the Indians themselves. This had always been a great wintering place for them."[1]

Under the treaty agreement, the Canadian government assumed responsibility to provide seed and materials to treaty Indians for farming the land. In the early years of reserve life (1876–79), however, this was not enough. There was malnutrition, even starvation, on many plains reserves. The government failed to provide an adequate administrative structure; often materials and seed stipulated in the contract were not sent. Many problems arose because a distant government in Ottawa simply did not understand the problems and conditions in the West. For example, in 1876 it was still possible for the minister of the interior, David Mills, to think that all Indians were on reserves. Policy decisions that restricted the ability of reserve residents to farm did not further the stated goal of making the Indians self-sufficient agriculturalists. It may well be that solving the very difficult problems faced by the Indians was simply beyond the insights and resources available to that generation of Whites. These problems were compounded when those starving Indians who had not initially signed treaties began to turn to the reserves as their hopes for subsistence from game on the plains waned.

Indian policy and the administration put in place to implement it originated in Ottawa. The earliest policies from the early 1870s were part of a process intended to settle Indians on reserves. The main task of the first two Boards of Commissions—in 1874 and 1876 respectively—had been to sign treaties with the Indians, especially in the fertile belt, where settlers were expected and encouraged to take up lands according to the National Policy. By 1876, with the treaty-making for the most part completed in the Cypress Hills area, changes were made to adapt to the duties that emerged. The Board of Commissions was replaced by a system of Indian superintendents with two or more Indian agents in each superintendency. Under this arrangement there were four superintendencies for the area between the Pacific Coast and the Ontario-Manitoba border; in the North-West Superintendency alone there were seventeen thousand treaty Indians to administer. The Indian agents had the least amount of time for farm instruction, which ironically was the task that the Indians required most.

The Indians were interested in learning about mechanized farming practices but complained that little teaching was available. In practice, they provided the farm instructors with free manual labor without any profit to themselves. Many of the farm instructors hired to assist in developing agricultural skills among the Indians proved to be sadly inept. Most had little farm experience and were unsuited to dealing with a society that was so different from their own. Tension and misunderstanding resulted.

The situation proved to be disastrous. The Indians had been encouraged to settle on reserves, but the agricultural policy the government was proposing was not able to provide them with enough food to survive. Many Indians who were willing to farm had to return to hunting to avoid starvation—precisely what the government had wanted to avoid. Money granted by the treaties proved to be grossly inadequate. There were not even sufficient resources to purchase enough food to provide basic nutrition. The lack of farm equipment also prevented farming beyond a very primitive level. Even when it was provided, the equipment usually came without adequate operating instructions. When it was broken, there was no way to repair it. In the end, much of the machinery remained virtually useless.

The instructors had been directed by Ottawa to implement a policy of "work for rations." This was resented by the Indians, who thought the rations were a right and not something to be earned. In Treaty 6 they pointed to the famine clause, as Indian culture demanded sharing with those in need and assistance to the sick. The Cree thought the Canadian government should share with them during times of starvation, just as the Cree had done for them in the past. The "work for rations" policy was intended to instill in the Indians the idea that rations could not be handed out but had to be earned by completing tasks. The Indians found this paternalism humiliating. They also saw little use in the menial work demanded of them.

With no relief from starvation on reserves in sight, the government recognized the need to revise their policies. In 1879 they began the Home Farm Plan, which was to provide examples of proper farming practices on model farms. Besides educating the Indians about farming, the farms were to provide them with enough food to prevent starvation and to supply seeds for future crops. Again, the policy was somewhat condescending and paternalistic. The program proved to be another failure as the Indians resented the free labor demanded of them; they wanted wages.

By 1882 Macdonald's government had begun to cut back all government programs, and the Home Farm Plan was one of the first casualties. This attempt at using model farms fizzled out dismally. There had been no proper and competent administration, and resources had been woefully inadequate. The problems of farming on reserves were a concern to government officials through the early 1880s, but the only solution provided was to send more farm instructors and Indian agents. In areas where there were no home farms, little was done to provide instruction beyond sending a farming instructor—if one was available. These were superficial solutions to what were becoming increasingly complex problems, and the Indians were beginning to give up on a government that, during the treaty process, had seemed so eager to assist them in adapting to agricultural life on the reserve.[2]

Two home farms had been established in 1879 in the Cypress Hills, one for the Cree and one for the Assiniboin. The home farm for the Assiniboin was established under the instructor John J. English and later became the Horace Greely Ranch. The other home farm was established forty-eight kilometers (30 mi) northeast of Fort Walsh on Maple Creek. Cowesses, or Little Child, had selected a reserve here, and members of his band settled in the area, although the official survey to establish the reserve was never completed. In 1881 Piapot chose a reserve about sixteen kilometers (10 mi) north of the Maple Creek farm.

The Maple Creek farm was supervised by John Setter, who, unlike most in the first contingent of farm instructors, was a "man of the country," a son of an HBC man, born at Red River. Agent McDonald reported that Setter had excellent crops after one year, considering that there had been no rain and that seeding had been completed late in the season. He noted that the Indians had displayed a "great deal of energy in trying to make a success of their first agricultural enterprize [sic]."[3] The following year there were

46.5 hectares (115 acres) of wheat, oats, turnips, and potatoes under cultivation at the Maple Creek farm. Some of the Indians were reported to be working at their farms remarkably well; they took considerable pride in their gardens and were annoyed that there was not more seed available. A number of them had planted wheat for themselves, and McDonald recommended that the Maple Creek farm be supplied with a portable grist mill. He believed that if the Indians could grind their grain, a large number of them could be induced to break land for the following year. He was confident that the Indians here could be self-sustaining in another year. Despite the fact that the home farm at Maple Creek proved to be one of the great successes of the program, it was closed in the winter of 1881–82 when the government decided to disallow reserves in the Cypress Hills and to move all treaty Indians in the area to reserves to the north or east.

Up until 1882, bands of Cree and Assiniboin who had not signed Treaties 4 and 6 congregated in the Cypress Hills. Game could still support the Indians in the area, but eventually the large numbers of Indians around Fort Walsh depleted these resources. In 1881 four thousand Indians were fed around Fort Walsh. The Indians' ranks become thinned when Piapot signed Treaty 4 in 1875 and when Little Pine signed Treaty 6 in 1879. Only Big Bear remained in the Cypress Hills, and with him the dream of establishing a large reserve. Big Bear hoped that a large concentration of Cree in the Cypress Hills might force the government into talks that could lead to the fulfillment of treaty promises. The Cree, however, were weakened by starvation and were unable to maintain a strong position in the Hills. Their forays into the United States in pursuit of the last buffalo herds were less and less successful as the American army was on the lookout to drive the Cree back into Canadian territory.

Big Bear's other hope—to forge an alliance with the Blackfoot and Crow peoples to prevent the destruction of the buffalo herds—was frustrated by the horse stealing that plagued peaceful relations among the tribes. Starving young warriors carried out these raids and leaders such as Big Bear were powerless to stop them. By late 1882, the same year the NWMP detachment was preparing to move from Fort Walsh to Maple Creek, Big Bear's band was racked with dissension. Many of his followers wanted to sign the treaty in order to receive rations. That year, as the band was camped around Cypress Lake, the decision was made to sign an adhesion to Treaty 6 and move north. Big Bear had no strength left to resist. In the north, Big Bear would once again work to unite the Cree in an unsuccessful effort to force the government to deliver on its treaty promises.

The government decision in the winter of 1881–82 to remove Indians from the Cypress Hills was born of fear. The usual explanation is that officials feared conflict or collusion between American and Canadian Indians and they wanted to discourage horse-stealing raids, which they feared might lead to international incidents. A more recent interpretation suggests, however, that Canadian authorities were concerned about the danger that might be posed by a concentration of the Cree on contiguous reserves in the Cypress Hills, as this would effectively create an Indian territory in which the residents would be difficult to control.

Thus, Commissioner of Indian Affairs Edgar Dewdney had been pursuing a policy of starving into submission those who had not signed the treaty because he feared a large concentration of Cree in the area. In 1882–83, the federal government announced new regulations that restricted the payment of annuities to Indians on reserves only, rationing was discontinued, and Fort Walsh was closed. In pursuing this action, Dewdney violated oral promises he had made in 1880 and 1881 to allow the Cree and Assiniboin reserves in the Hills. His denial of a reserve in the Cypress Hills to Big Bear was also a violation of written promises made by the Treaty Commissions of both 1874 and 1876.

There was one Indian band, however, that refused to move. Foremost Man, or Nekaneet, insisted on taking his reserve in the Cypress Hills area. After Nekaneet signed Treaty 4, he took his annuity payments at Fort Qu'Appelle, then, in 1879, he began to take payment at Fort Walsh. Even after others in his band had settled in the Qu'Appelle area, Nekaneet remained on the plains around the Cypress Hills with other independent Cree. In 1881, Nekaneet and his band ranged as far south as the Missouri River before American authorities intercepted, disarmed, and escorted them back to Canada.

After the winter of 1882–83, when the new government regulations about annuity payments were introduced and rationing was discontinued, many Indians left Nekaneet's band to settle on reserves away from the Hills. These actions did not discourage the most committed of Nekaneet's band, however, even though the number of band members declined from 428 in 1881, to 350 in 1883, and to 119 in 1898. Even when Fort Walsh was abandoned in 1883, and the NWMP detachment moved to Maple Creek, the Cree continued to stay in the Cypress Hills.

In these years Nekaneet continued to press his claims for a reserve in the Hills:

> I have been born and have lived in this part of the country where I was raised in. I have always been a loyal subject to Her Majesty's Government and whenever I meet white People I

have always been friendly to them. I showed my loyalty when there was trouble in 1885 by keeping my Band quiet."[4]

Through the 1890s, the Canadian government continually attempted to induce the Indians to settle on reserves. Many tactics were used. Hayter Reed, eventually deputy superintendent of Indian Affairs, tried to label Foremost Man's band as troublemakers, even though there was little evidence of this and their relations with the local White community were good. The Indians in his band never asked for government assistance. One police officer observed: "If we do not happen to find out their condition they will say nothing as they are morbidly afraid of accepting assistance from the government least they should be compelled to go and live on a reserve. One is disposed to think that life on any kind of reserve must be better than the life they lead, but they cannot be persuaded to think so."[5]

Nekaneet died in 1897 before his dream of a reserve in the Cypress Hills was realized. The Canadian government finally relented and granted the descendants of Nekaneet's band a reserve in 1913, giving it his name. It was not until 1975 that the government agreed to pay the band its treaty benefits, after they had lived without them for ninety-three years.

INDIAN WOMEN ON RESERVES

Starvation was constantly on the horizon for the Indians as their lifestyles changed, and women became an essential economic component of reserve life by learning new skills and adapting old ones. Their adaptability helped diversify the food supply and contributed to risk-reduction for fragile reserve economies. The hard work of women was not their only contribution. They were also a spiritual inspiration to their communities. As one Cree observer noted: "Theirs was the satisfaction of making their loved ones happy. Their cheerfulness could not help but be infectious, thus everyone was soon striving to do his share and the Crees were able to look on the bright side of things."[6]

Restricted movement meant that foraging activities were not conducted over as large an area as they had once been; nevertheless wild fruits remained a staple and included saskatoons, wild raspberries and strawberries, black currants, and choke cherries. Wild rhubarb was used in soups and kinnikinnik was gathered as a tobacco substitute. Sap from birch and maple trees was boiled and manufactured into syrup. Roots such as wild turnip were collected and dried. Seneca root was collected for trade, as well as for home use as a medicine. Fish were caught and smoked by women throughout the spring and summer. Wild fowl were caught, plucked, and dried as were other small game such as rabbit, prairie chicken, and gopher.

Much of the work of collecting, hunting, and food preparation was done communally, and the activities and excursions were characterized by a spirit of high morale and humor.

Hauling water and wood were the daily heavy work done by women to maintain their households. Offsetting this hard work was the weaving—more commonly done in winter—when hats and baskets were made out of rushes and willows that had been collected in the warmer months. Clothes were made and repaired throughout the year but more commonly in winter months. Other, more labor-intensive, work was grinding grain into flour and the continual tanning of hides.

Many of these activities changed little from pre-reserve days, but there were new forms of labor undertaken by women during the reserve era. Many of these were associated with agriculture. Working in grain fields, stooking, gathering, and binding sheaves were all new skills the women had to learn. Other skills adapted for the reserve era that required women's labor included butter making, milking, bread making, knitting, mending, soap making, gardening, caring for poultry, and calving. As well, women were often called upon to make repairs to huts or cabins that had been built from poor lumber that often provided only the barest of shelter. Reserve poverty left most families with minimal housing:

> ... low, one-storey, one-room log structures with mud roofs and wood fireplaces. Many had flooring by the late 1880s, but few had amenities such as glass windows, banks or bedsteads, cooking stoves, chairs, dishes, and coal lamps. The open fireplace, made of upright posts covered with a thick coating of clay mixed with water, provided both heat and light. The chimney, always open, served as ventilator. The sleeping places were seldom more than a bundle of rags on the floor.[7]

The conditions that women had to cope with in their homes was as bad as the poor anywhere had to contend with. But they managed to survive, as many have noted, with a resiliency and often with humor.

RANCHING

The cattle industry in the Cypress Hills began with the NWMP herds that were brought in to feed starving Indians between 1879 and 1883. The cattle were brought to Fort Walsh from the south through contracts for beef with the I. G. Baker Co. Before the disappearance of the buffalo there had been no cattle to speak of because on the open range bulls were killed by the buffalo bulls and the cows would drift off with the buffalo herds.

The first cattle ranchers in the Cypress Hills settled near the fort in the years before the CPR passed through Maple Creek in 1883. The first ranchers close to the site of Fort Walsh were Wellington Anderson and David Wood. They brought their cattle out from Manitoba in the early 1890s on a drive that took them two months. The pair remained partners for twenty-five years. A number of other ranches, including those of the Lawrences and Pollocks, were established in the 1880s and 1890s. John Linder, born in Germany, brought twenty head of cattle and ten horses to the Fort Walsh area. He and his four sons occupied an enormous expanse of leased land extending over seventy-two sections. Everett Parsonage from England homesteaded just south of Battle Creek, and James Gaff came from Kansas and Nebraska before settling next to the Linder place. Eventually ranch homes were dotted along all the creeks flowing north and south from the Cypress Hills: Fish Creek, Piapot Creek, Bear Creek, Battle Creek, and Skull Creek.

The settlers were from a wide variety of backgrounds and included a number of Métis families. John Laframboise and his family established themselves at Piapot Creek in the mid-1880s. Jules Quesnell, who had herded cattle for the I. G. Baker Co., worked for a time on the Oxarart Ranch and settled at Hay Creek, as did Celistine St. Denis. Francis Xavier Swain, who was married to Mary Breland (great-granddaughter of the Métis leader Cuthbert Grant),[8] settled in the Skull Creek district. An Indian from Manitoba, John Tanner, who once ran mail for the NWMP, also tried to establish a farm in the Hills, but as a treaty Indian he was not allowed to homestead.

There were a number of famous large ranches in the area, including the Oxarart Ranch, which was established in the early 1880s near Battle Creek. The owners were Basques from the Pyrenees who brought three hundred head of horses with them and took out leases for a 4048-hectare (10,000-acre) grazing area. They imported thoroughbred horses from England and the United States and owned the famous race horse "Blair Athol," who was ridden by John Léveillé. The Léveillé brothers were the cowboys on this ranch, which grew to have a herd of 1,700 that at one time grazed an area that was said to have run from the Cypress Hills to the Milk River and the Alberta border to Val Marie. Other large ranches at the turn of the century were those of the Pollock Brothers, the Cheeseman Brothers, the Dixon Brothers, and Horace Greely. It was not until 1906 that farmers were attracted to the area and began to change the way of life. The property on which Fort Walsh stands was sold to the RCMP by Frank Nuttall in 1942. There the police established a remount station to train and raise horses. The Mounties reconstructed a number of buildings from 1943 to 1967; many of the structures reconstructed were based on those in the original fort.

FORT WALSH AS A NATIONAL HISTORIC SITE

Fort Walsh was dismantled and abandoned in 1883. By the 1890s the site had become the headquarters for the Wood and Anderson ranching operation. Ranching activity continued on the site until the early 1940s, when the RCMP acquired the property and constructed a remount ranch on the site of the original fort to breed horses for the force's equestrian training and the famous Musical Ride. When the RCMP remount operation was moved to Ontario in 1968, the property was transferred to the Canadian Parks Service.

In 1972 Fort Walsh was formally declared a national historic site, encompassing a land base of 650 hectares (1,605 acres), which makes it one of the larger sites in the national system of historic parks and sites. Despite this relatively recent designation as a national historic site, Fort Walsh had been declared a site of national historic significance by the Historic Sites and Monuments Board of Canada in 1924. This was followed in 1926 by the erection of a commemorative plaque and cairn to recognize Fort Walsh as a center of law and order in the Canadian West. In 1964 the Historic Sites and Monuments Board further recommended that the Cypress Hills Massacre be recognized as an event of national significance "because of its influence on the passage of the bill to establish the North-West Mounted Police."[9] During Canada's Centennial in 1967, the Board reinforced the significance of Fort Walsh by recommending that its founder and commander, James Morrow Walsh, be commemorated as an "eminent Canadian."

Since 1968, the Canadian Parks Service has gradually developed a visitor program and maintenance operation at Fort Walsh National Historic Site that is centered upon the reconstructed buildings of the fort and Farwell's and Solomon's trading posts. In 1976 the Canadian Parks Service opened a visitor reception center with an exhibit hall, audio-visual theater, and food services, an internal transportation system, and a seasonal staff of interpreters who present the Fort Walsh story through tours and special programs. The operation of the park, which is open to the public from mid-May to Thanksgiving, is supported by a small administrative staff based in Maple Creek, Saskatchewan. Each National Historic Site represents some aspect of Canadian history. Their theme statements provide the historic rationale and national context for the planning and development of an historic site so that its resources are conserved, commemorated, managed, and interpreted in an appropriate manner. Three primary themes—Native People in the Cypress Hills; Whoop-Up Country and the Cypress Hills Massacre; The NWMP and Canadian Sovereignty in the Northwest—and one secondary theme—Ranching and the Remount Station Era—have been identified to present the story of the fort in the Cypress Hills in a comprehensive historic context.[10]

NOTES

Chapter Two: Buffalo and the Fur Trade

1   Alexander Henry the Elder, *Travels and Adventures in Canada*, pp. 299–300.
2   Glyndwr Williams, "The Hudson's Bay Company and the Fur Trade," p. 35.
3   Ibid., p. 42.
4   John Milloy, *The Plains Cree*, p. 186.
5   Eleanor Burke Leacock, "Montagnais Women."
6   Alan Michael Klein, "Adaptive Strategies on the Plains."

Chapter Three: Whoop-Up Country

1   E. E. Rich, *The Fur Trade*, p. 240.
2   John E. Sunder, *The Fur Trade on the Upper Missouri*, p. 258.
3   T. Lindsay Baker, "Beaver to Buffalo Robes," no. 2, p. 6.
4   Margaret Anne Kennedy and Brian O. K. Reeves, *An Inventory of Whiskey Posts*, vol. I, pp. 27–28; Paul F. Sharp, *Whoop-Up Country*, pp. 44–45.
5   Georgia G. Fooks, "Fort Whoop-Up," p. 6.
6   Paul F. Sharp, *Whoop-Up Country*, pp. 48–49.
7   Abel Farwell, Inventory Ledgers.
8   Henry C. Klassen, "International Enterprise," p. 58; and James M. Francis, "Montana Business," p. 292.
9   Rhoda R. Gilman, "The Upper Mississippi Fur Trade," p. 123. Gilman noted the number and value of furs sold in the U.S. actually increased from 1830 to 1870.
10   T. Lindsay Baker, "Beaver to Buffalo Robes," no. 2, p. 6; Georgia G. Fooks, "Fort Whoop-Up," p. 23; and "Paid to Hammond, June 6, 1872," T. C. Power Papers, Box 277, Folder 8.
11   T. Lindsay Baker, "Beaver to Buffalo Robes," no. 2, p. 6.
12   Ibid., p. 11.
13   Robson Bonnichsen and Stuart J. Baldwin, "Cypress Hills," App. 3, p. 77.
14   Jacqueline Peterson, "Many Roads to Red River," pp. 38–39.
15   Andy Den Otter, "Transportation, Trade and Regional Identity," p. 4.
16   Clovis Rondeau, *La Montagne de Bois*, pp. 10–11.
17   Ibid., p. 11.
18   Ibid., p. 15.
19   Isaac Cowie, *The Company of Adventurers*, pp. 431 and 462. Cowie believed the establishment of his post led other traders and Indians to violate what he thought was the traditional neutrality of the Hills to exploit its animal resources.

20 Ibid., pp. 432–37.
21 Paul F. Sharp, *Whoop-Up Country*, p. 39.
22 Gerald L. Berry, *The Whoop-Up Trail*, pp. 39–41; Margaret Anne Kennedy and Brian O. K. Reeves, *An Inventory of Whiskey Posts*, vol. I, pp. 13–14; and Georgia G. Fooks, "Fort Whoop-Up," p. 38.
23 Paul C. Phillips, "The Fur Trade in Montana," p. 60.
24 Paul F. Sharp, *Merchant Princes*, pp. 7–9.
25 James M. Francis, "Montana Business," p. 296.
26 Ibid., pp. 292–93.
27 Henry C. Klassen, "I. G. Baker," p. 42.
28 Henry C. Klassen, "International Enterprise," p. 292.
29 Peter Darby, "River Boats to Rail Lines," p. 13.
30 Dr. John E. Foster, personal communication, January 8, 1992.
31 Margaret Anne Kennedy and Brian O. K. Reeves, *An Inventory of Whiskey Posts*, vol. I, p. 15.
32 Peter Darby, "River Boats to Rail Lines," p. 13.
33 Margaret Anne Kennedy, "A Whiskey Trade Frontier," pp. 59–60.
34 Francis Paul Prucha, *Indian Policy*, p. 72.
35 Paul F. Sharp, *Merchant Princes*, p. 5; and Henry C. Klassen, "I. G. Baker," p. 43.
36 Mary L. Weeks, *The Last Buffalo Hunter*, p. 153.
37 Paul F. Sharp, *Whoop-Up Country*, p. 42; Margaret Anne Kennedy and Brian O. K. Reeves, *An Inventory of Whiskey Posts*, vol. I, p. 14; and Georgia G. Fooks, "Fort Whoop-Up," p. 2.
38 Brian Hubner, "'The Farwellians.'"
39 Hugh A. Dempsey, "Sweet Grass Hills Massacre," p. 13; and Henry C. Klassen, "International Enterprise," p. 42.
40 Lewis O. Saum, "From Vermont to Whoop-Up Country," p. 57; and Dan L. Tharpp, *Encyclopedia of Frontier Biography*, "J. J. Healy," vol. II, p. 637.
41 Paul F. Sharp, *Merchant Princes*, p. 5. Sharp claimed the trade was built "out of ruins" of the American Fur Company.
42 Margaret Anne Kennedy and Brian O. K. Reeves, *An Inventory of Whiskey Posts*, vol. II, p. 171; Dan L. Tharpp, *Encyclopedia of Frontier Biography*, "Joe Kipp," vol. II, pp. 787–88; D. B. Sealy, "Jerry Potts," *Dictionary of Canadian Biography*, vol. 12, pp. 858–59.
43 Margaret Anne Kennedy, "A Whiskey Trade Frontier," p. 65.
44 W. Henry McKay, "The Story of Edward McKay," pp. 76–77, 100–01, and 105.
45 Margaret Anne Kennedy, "A Whiskey Trade Frontier," p. 310.
46 Margaret Anne Kennedy and Brian O. K. Reeves, *An Inventory of Whiskey Posts*, vol. I, p. ii; Jack Elliott, "Tradition and Fact," p. 19; and Philip

Goldring, "Whiskey, Horses and Death," p. 47. Goldring stated that there were thirteen traders, in 1873 in the Cypress Hills, operating within a 4.8-kilometer (3-mi) radius.

47 A. B. McCullough, Papers, pp. 9–10.

Chapter Four: The Cypress Hills Massacre

1 This is based on the 1870 U.S. census, which included a twenty-eight-year-old Abel Farwell, born in Massachusetts, living in Dawson County; and a thirty-six-year-old A. C. Farwell, born in New York, and living in Fort Benton. These two Farwells may actually refer to the same person as the Dawson County census was done at a later date. Joel Overholser, letter of August 25, 1983. The whole issue is confused by Farwell's statement in 1876 that he was thirty-eight years old and so born around 1838. The *Winnipeg Standard,* June 24, 1876; and Philip Goldring, *Whisky, Horses and Death,* p. 47.

2 George Lande, taped interview, April 10, 1991; and The *Winnipeg Standard,* June 24, 1876.

3 Anon., "Old Fort Peck," p. 2.

4 Abel Farwell Inventory Ledgers for 1869, 1870, 1871, pp. 72–74 and 1872 "Petty Ledger 'D'; Abel Farwell, 'Cypress Mountains'; and Isaac Cowie, *The Company of Adventurers,* p. 388.

5 Margaret Anne Kennedy, personal communication, December 7, 1989; and Margaret Anne Kennedy and Brian O. K. Reeves, *An Inventory of Whiskey Posts,* vol. I, p. 73.

6 Margaret Anne Kennedy, "A Whiskey Trade Frontier," pp. 251–52.

7 Hugh A. Dempsey, "Sweet Grass Hills Massacre," pp. 14–15.

8 Jack Elliott, "Tradition and Fact," pp. 8–9 and 15–17.

9 The *Helena Daily Independent,* "The Extradition Trial," July 15, 1875; and George Lande, taped interview, April 10, 1991.

10 Bureau of Indian Affairs, file 30 SA.

11 Hammond/Coombes/Beckwith, "Family Genealogy."

12 L. J. Hammond, "Certificate of Membership."

13 Joel Overholser, personal communication, December 14, 1989.

14 Bob Saindon and Bunky Sullivan, "Taming the Missouri," p. 36.

15 Anon., *Progressive Men of Montana,* p. 1678.

16 Georgia G. Fooks, "Fort Whoop-Up," pp. 7–8.

17 Charles Rowe, "The Bluff of Fred Kanouse."

18 T. C. Power Papers, June 6, 1872.

19 Dan Kennedy, *Recollection of an Assiniboine Chief,* p. 42.

20 Philip Goldring, *Whisky, Horses and Death,* p. 47; and The *Winnipeg Standard,* June 24, 1876.

21 Anon., *Progressive Men of Montana,* p. 1678; and 1900 U.S. Census.

118

22   Hazel Jacobsen, *Profile of Early Ovando,* pp. 49–50.
23   T. R. McCloy, "The descendants"; and personal communication, July 10, 1990.
24   Philip Goldring, *Whisky, Horses and Death,* p. 47; The *Winnipeg Standard,* June 24, 1879; and Joel Overholser, personal communication, June 25, 1991.
25   This is the description of Solomon by his granddaughter, who knew him. Winniefred Eastlund Arhelger, "Moses Salomon," p. 2.
26   The name was usually written Solomon or Soloman, although he was born Salomon, and the first name was rendered as Moses or Mose.
27   Winniefred Eastlund Arhelger, "Moses Salomon," p. 1.
28   Joel Overholser, *Fort Benton,* pp. 145–47; and *The Kendall Miner,* "Tribute to His Memory," August 31, 1906, in Winniefred Eastlund Arhelger, "Moses Salomon," p. 4.
29   Moses Solomon was first mentioned at Fort Benton in 1865. Joel Overholser, personal communication, November 3, 1989.
30   The *River Press,* September 5, 1906; and Jim Wood, personal communication, August 9, 1922. Solomon traveled to Fort Peck in 1866 in a mackinaw and he appears on a Deer Lodge passenger list.
31   T. C. Power Papers, Petty Ledger "A" 1867–70, "H" 1869–70, "D" 1872–74, "B" 1870–72, #2 1869, "C" 1871–72. Solomon purchased supplies from T. C. Power in the period 1867–74.
32   Margaret Anne Kennedy and Brian O. K. Reeves, *An Inventory of Whiskey Posts,* vol. I, p. 124.
33   Jack Elliott, "Tradition and Fact," pp. 7–8, 17, 19, and 40.
34   Philip Goldring, *Whisky, Horses and Death,* p. 47.
35   Hugh A. Dempsey, "Sweet Grass Hills Massacre," pp. 12–18; and Joel Overholser, personal communication, November 3, 1989.
36   Philip Goldring, *Whisky, Horses and Death,* p. 51
37   Ibid., p. 53.
38   Ibid.
39   Ibid.
40   The *Winnipeg Standard,* June 24, 1876.
41   Philip Goldring, *Whisky, Horses and Death,* p. 56.

Chapter Five: Fort Walsh and the Mounties

1   Edwin Charles Morgan, *North-West Mounted Police,* pp. 92–93.
2   A. Wilson, *The Letters of Charles John Brydges,* p. 47.
3   Ibid., p. 37.
4   Ibid., p. 157. Smith and Kavanaugh were competing tenderers for government contracts.
5   T. C. Powers Papers, 55–106–9, January 27, 1880.
6   Wallace E. Stegner, *Wolf Willow,* p. 303.
7   John Turner, *The North-West Mounted Police,* vol. I, p. 496.

Chapter Six: Treaties and Reservations

1   John Milloy, *The Plains Cree* and Arthur Ray, *Indians in the Fur Trade.*
2   John Milloy, *The Plains Cree,* pp. 266–67.
3   Frederick Turner, *Beyond Geography.*
4   Irene Spry, "From a Nomadic to a Settled Economy," p. 204.
5   Ibid., p. 205.
6   Ibid., p. 211.
7   Gerald Friesen, *The Canadian Prairies,* p. 20.
8   Sarah Carter, *Lost Harvests,* p. 54.
9   Ibid., p. 55.
10   Ibid.
11   Ibid., p. 56.
12   Ibid., p. 57.
13   Ibid., p. 58.
14   Robert Utley, *The Lance and the Shield,* pp. 14–15, 22.
15   John Peter Turner, *The North-West Mounted Police,* vol. I, p. 290.
16   John S. Gray, *Custer's Last Campaign,* pp. 373–400.
17   Ellen McLeod, *Fort Walsh,* pp. 39–44.
18   John Peter Turner, *The North-West Mounted Police,* vol. I, p. 364.
19   Ibid., p. 468.
20   Grant MacEwan, "Sitting Bull." *Dictionary of Canadian Biography,* vol. 11, p. 870.
21   John Peter Turner, *The North-West Mounted Police,* vol. I, p. 587.
22   Grant MacEwan, "Sitting Bull." *Dictionary of Canadian Biography,* vol. 11, p. 870.
23   Ibid.
24   William A. Waiser, "The North-West Mounted Police."

Chapter Seven: The Modern Age

1   John Peter Turner, *The North-West Mounted Police,* vol. I, pp. 508–59.
2   Sarah Carter, *Lost Harvests,* Chap. 2.
3   Ibid., p. 179.
4   David Lee, "Foremost Man and His Band," p. 97. Nekaneet's band did not join the Cree in the 1885 Rebellion.
5   Ibid., p. 112.
6   Sarah Carter, *Lost Harvests,* p. 177.
7   Ibid., p. 179.
8   Cuthbert Grant led the Métis against the governor of Red River, Robert Semple, at the Battle of Seven Oaks in 1816.
9   Although the Act was in place at the time of the massacre, it had not yet been enacted.
10   Anon., "Fort Walsh Management Plan."

BIBLIOGRAPHY

Abel, Annie Heloise, ed. *Chardon's Journal at Fort Clarke 1834–1839.* Pierre: Department of History, State of South Dakota, 1932.

Anon., "Old Fort Peck." In *Fort Peck, A Job Well Done, Oct. 1933–Aug. 1977.* Fort Peck Reunion Committee. Glasgow: Ne Mont Printer, 1977.

Anon., "Fort Walsh Management Plan." Winnipeg: Canadian Parks Service, 1992.

Anon., "The Fort Benton and Fort Sarpy Journal, 1855–1856." Contributions to the Historical Society of Montana, vol. 10, 1940. Helena: Naegele Printing Co., 1940.

Anon., *Epitome of Parliamentary Documents in Connection with the North-West Rebellion, 1885.* Ottawa: Maclean, Roger & Co., 1886.

Anon., *Progressive Men of Montana.* Chicago: A. W. Bowen & Co., 1903.

Arhelger, Winniefred Eastlund. "Moses Salomon," ms., 1990. Fort Walsh National Historic Site library, Maple Creek, Saskatchewan.

Audubon, John J. *Audubon and His Journals,* vol. I. Edited by Maria R. Audubon. New York: Dover Pub., 1960 ed.

Baker, T. Lindsay. "Beaver to Buffalo Robes: Transition in the Fur Trade." *The Museum of the Fur Trade Quarterly* 23, nos. 1 & 2 (Spring and Summer 1987): 1–8, 4–13.

Berry, Gerald L. *The Whoop-Up Trail: Early Days in Alberta-Montana.* Edmonton: Applied Art Products Ltd., 1953.

Bonnichsen, Robson and Baldwin, Stuart J. "Cypress Hills Ethnohistory and Ecology," Archaeological Survey of Alberta, Occasional Paper No. 10. Edmonton: Alberta Culture and Historical Resources, 1978.

Bureau of Indian Affairs files. Crow Agency, Montana.

Cardiff, Daryl. "The Diplomatic Imbroglio Over the Sioux in Canada and the Terry Commission of 1877," ms., 1990. University of Lethbridge, Lethbridge, Alberta.

Carter, Sarah. *Lost Harvests: Prairie Reserve Farmers and Government Policy.* Montreal: McGill-Queen's University Press, 1990.

The Commissioners of the Royal North-West Mounted Police. *Opening Up The West, 1874–1881; Being The Official Reports To Parliament Of The Activities Of The Royal North-West Mounted Police Force, from 1874–1881.* Toronto: Coles Publishing Co., Toronto, 1973.

The Commissioners of the Royal North-West Mounted Police. *Settlers and Rebels, 1882–1885; Being The Official Reports To Parliament Of The Activities Of The Royal North-West Mounted Police Force, from 1874–1881.* Toronto: Coles Publishing Co., 1973.

Cowie, Isaac. *The Company of Adventurers: A Narrative of Seven Years in the*

Service of the Hudson's Bay Company During 1867–1874 on the Great Buffalo Plains. Toronto: William Briggs, 1913.

Darby, Peter. "From River Boats to Rail Lines: Circulation Patterns in the Canadian West during the Last Quarter of the Nineteenth Century." In *Essays in the Historical Geography of the Canadian West: Regional Perspectives of the Settlement Process*, pp. 5–26. Edited by L. A. Rosenvall and S. M. Evans. Calgary: University of Calgary, Geography Dept., 1987.

Dempsey, Hugh A. "Cypress Hills Massacre." *Montana the Magazine of Western History* 3, no. 4 (Autumn 1953): 1–9.

Dempsey, Hugh A. "Sweet Grass Hills Massacre." *Montana the Magazine of Western History* 7, no. 2 (April 1957): 12–18.

Den Otter, Andy. "Transportation, Trade and Regional Identity in the Southwestern Prairies." *Prairie Forum* 15, no. 1 (Spring 1990): 1–23.

Denig, Edwin Thompson. *Five Tribes of the Upper Missouri: Sioux, Arickaras, Assiniboines, Crees, Crows.* Norman: University of Oklahoma Press, 1973.

Elliott, Jack. "Tradition and Fact—Archaeological Examination of the Cypress Hills Massacre." National Historic Service Report No. 86. Ottawa: Manuscript NHSS Series, 1972.

Ewers, John C. *The Blackfeet: Raiders of the Northwest Plains.* Norman: University of Oklahoma, 1958.

Farwell, Abel. Inventory Ledgers for 1869, 1870, 1871 and 1872. "Life in Whoop-Up Country" file. Fort Walsh National Historic Site Library, Maple Creek, Saskatchewan.

Fooks, Georgia G. "Fort Whoop-Up—Alberta's First and Most Notorious Whiskey Fort." Whoop-Up Country Chapter, Historical Society of Alberta Occasional Paper No. 11. Lethbridge: Historical Society of Alberta, 1983.

Foster, John E. Personal communication, January 8, 1992. Edmonton, Alberta.

Francis, James M. "Montana Business and Canadian Regionalism in the 1870s and 1880s." *The Western Historical Quarterly* 12 (July 1981): 291–304.

Friesen, Gerald. *The Canadian Prairies: A History.* Toronto: University of Toronto Press, 1984.

Gilman, Rhoda R. "Last Days of the Upper Mississippi Fur Trade." *Minnesota History* 42 (1970): 122–40.

Goldring, Philip. *Whisky, Horses and Death: The Cypress Hills Massacre and its Sequel.* Occasional Papers in Archaeology and History No. 21. Ottawa: National Historic Service, 1973.

Gray, John S. *Custer's Last Campaign: Mitch Boyer and the Little Bighorn Reconstructed.* Lincoln: University of Nebraska Press, 1991.

Hammond, L. J. Personal communication, April 15, 1991. Deer Lodge, Montana.

Hammond, L. J. "Certificate of Membership—Sons and Daughters of Montana Pioneers," Deer Lodge, Montana.

Hammond/Coombes/Beckwith "Family Genealogy." Courtesy of L. J. Hammond, Deer Lodge, Montana.

Bibliography

Healy, John J. "Bucking The Hudson Bay Company. Told by Captain John J. Healy. Written by Forrest Crissey." The *Saturday Evening Post*, pp. 15–17, June 20, 1903.

Henry, Alexander the Elder, *Travels and Adventures in Canada and the Indian Territories Between the Years 1760–1776.* Edited by James Bain. Toronto: George N. Morany, 1901.

Hubner, Brian. "'The Farwellians': Collected Biographical Information on Persons Associated with Farwell's Post, 1872–1873," ms., 1991. Fort Walsh National Historic Site, Maple Creek, Saskatchewan.

Jacobsen, Hazel, comp. and ed. *Profile of Early Ovando, 1878–1900 (the recollections of Wilda Lynn Mannix).* Deer Lodge, Montana: Platen Press, 1977.

Kehoe, Thomas F. *The Gull Lake Site: A Prehistoric Bison Drive Site in South Western Saskatchewan.* Publications in Anthropology and History No. 1, Milwaukee Public Museum, 1973.

Kelson, Benjamin. "The Jews of Montana. Chapter I: Settlers in the Early Period, 1862–1885." *Western States Jewish Historical Quarterly* 3, no. 3 (April 1971): 170–85.

Kennedy, Dan. *Recollections of an Assiniboine Chief.* Edited by J. R. Stevens. Toronto: McClelland and Stewart, 1972.

Kennedy, Margaret Anne. Personal communication, December 7, 1989.

Kennedy, Margaret Anne. "A Whiskey Trade Frontier on the Northwestern Plains." Ph.D. thesis, University of Calgary, 1991.

Kennedy, Margaret Anne and Reeves, Brian O. K. *An Inventory and Historical Description of Whiskey Posts in Southern Alberta.* 2 vols. Edmonton: Historic Sites Service, Alberta Culture ms., 1984.

Klassen, Henry C. "I. G. Baker and Company in Calgary, 1875–1884." *Montana the Magazine of Western History* 35 (Summer 1985): 40–54.

Klassen, Henry C. "International Enterprise: The House of T. C. Power & Bro. in the Cypress Hills Trade, 1875–1893." *Saskatchewan History* 43 (Spring 1991): 57–71.

Klein, Alan Michael. "Adaptive Strategies and Process on the Plains: The 19th Century Cultural Sink." Ph.D. thesis, State University of New York, Buffalo, 1977.

Lande, George. Personal communication, July 9, 1990. Pryor, Montana.

Lande, George. Taped interview, April 10, 1991. Pryor, Montana.

Leacock, Eleanor Burke. "Montagnais Women and the Jesuit Program for Colonization." In *Rethinking Canada: The Promise of Women's History.* Edited by Veronica Strong-Boag and Anita Clair Fellman. Toronto: Copp Clarke Pitman, 1986.

Lee, David. "Foremost Man and His Band." *Saskatchewan History* 36, no. 3 (Autumn 1983): 94–101.

Leveillie, Gabriel. "Transcript of Tape Recording made by Gabriel (Gab)

Bibliography

Leveillie at Maple Creek Detachment, February 14th, 1957. Interviewed by Inspector T. E. Mudiman, O/C Swift Current Sub-Division." Medicine Hat Museum and Art Gallery Archives, Medicine Hat, Alberta.

Limmerick, Patricia Nelson. *The Legacy of Conquest. The Unbroken Past of the American West.* New York: W. W. Norton & Co., 1987.

McCloy, T. R. ". . . the descendants of John McKay and Mary Favell . . .," ms., 1983 ed. Medicine Hat Museum and Art Gallery Archives, Medicine Hat, Alberta.

McCloy, T. R. Personal communication, October 24, 1989, and July 10, 1990. Calgary, Alberta.

McCullough, A. B. Papers Relating to the North-West Mounted Police and Fort Walsh. Manuscript Report Number 213. Ottawa: Parks Canada, Department of Indian and Native Affairs, 1977.

McDougall, John. *On Western Trails in the Early Seventies: Frontier Life in the Canadian North-West.* Toronto: W. Biggs, 1911.

MacEwan, Grant. "Sitting Bull." In *Dictionary of Canadian Biography,* vol. 11. Toronto: University of Toronto Press, p. 870.

McKay, W. Henry. "The Story of Edward McKay." *Canadian Cattlemen* 10, no. 2 (September 1947): 76–77, 100–01 and 105.

McLeod, C. H. Papers. University of Montana Archives, Missoula, Montana.

McLeod, Ellen. *Fort Walsh, Saskatchewan.* National Historic Sites Service, Manuscript Report Number 62. Ottawa: National and Historic Parks Branch, 1969.

Milloy, John S. *The Plains Cree: Trade, Diplomacy and War, 1790–1870.* Manitoba Studies in Native History IV. Winnipeg: The University of Manitoba Press, 1988.

Morgan, Edwin Charles. *North-West Mounted Police, 1873–1883.* National Historic Parks and Sites Branch, Manuscript Report Number 113. Ottawa: Parks Canada, 1970.

Morice, Adrian Gabriel. *Dictionnaire historique des Canadiens et des Métis français de l'ouest.* Québec: J. P. Garneau, 1908.

Morris, Alexander. *The Treaties of Canada with the Indians of Manitoba and the Northwest Territories, Including the Negotiations on Which They Were Based, and Other Information Relating Thereto.* Toronto: Willing and Williamson, 1880.

Overholser, Joel. Letter, August 25, 1983, "Life in Whoop-Up Country" file. Fort Walsh National Historic Site Library, Maple Creek, Saskatchewan.

Overholser, Joel. Personal communication of September 26, 1989; November 3, 1989; December 14, 1989; June 25, 1991; and September 26, 1991. Fort Benton, Montana.

Overholser, Joel. *Fort Benton: World's Innermost Port.* Fort Benton: Joel Overholser, 1987.

Perry, Richard. "The Fur Trade and the Status of Women in the Western Subartic." *Ethnohistory* 26, no. 4 (Fall 1979): 363–75.

Peterson, Jacqueline. "Many Roads to Red River: Metis Genesis in the Great Lakes Region." In *The New Peoples: Being and Becoming Metis in North America,* edited by Jacqueline Peterson and Jennifer S. H. Brown. Manitoba Studies in Native History I. Winnipeg: University of Manitoba Press, 1985.

Phillips, Paul C. "The Fur Trade in Montana." In *The Montana Past: An Anthology.* Edited by Michael P. Malone and Richard B. Roeder. Missoula: University of Montana Press, 1969.

Power, Thomas C. Papers. Montana Historical Society, Helena, Montana.

Prucha, Francis Paul. *Indian Policy in the United States: Historical Essays.* Lincoln: University of Nebraska Press, 1981.

Ray, Arthur. *Indians in the Fur Trade: Their Role as Hunters, Trappers and Middlemen in the Lands southwest of Hudson's Bay, 1660–1870.* Toronto: University of Toronto Press, 1974.

Rich, E. E. *The Fur Trade and the Northwest to 1857.* Toronto: McClelland and Stewart, 1967.

Rondeau, Clovis. *La Montagne de Bois (Willow Bunch, Sask.): Histoire de la Saskatchewan meridionale.* Québec: L'Action Sociale, 1923.

Rowe, Charles. "The Bluff of Fred Kanouse." In *Rowe Family History,* n.d. pp. 80–83. Courtesy Joel Overholser, Fort Benton, Montana.

Saindon, Bob, and Sullivan, Bunky. "Taming the Missouri and Treating the Depression: Fort Peck Dam." *Montana the Magazine of Western History* 27, no. 3 (July 1977).

Saum, Lewis O. "From Vermont to Whoop-Up Country: Some Letters of D. W. Davis." *Montana the Magazine of Western History* 35 (Summer 1985): 56–71.

Sealy, D. B. "Jerry Potts," In *Dictionary of Canadian Biography,* vol. 12. Toronto: University of Toronto Press, 1990.

Sharp, Paul F. *Merchant Princes of the Plains.* Montana Heritage Series No. 5. Helena: Montana Historical Society Press, 1955.

Sharp, Paul F. *Whoop-Up Country: The Canadian-American West, 1865–1885.* Minneapolis: University of Minnesota Press, 1955.

Spry, Irene. "The Transition from a Nomadic to a Settled Economy in Western Canada, 1856–96." Transactions of the Royal Society of Canada fourth series, vol. 6 (1968): 203–29.

Steele, Samuel B. *Forty Years in Canada.* New York: Dodd, Mead and Company, 1915.

Stegner, Wallace E. *Wolf Willow; a History, a Story, and a Memory of the Last Plains Frontier.* Toronto: Macmillan of Canada, 1955.

Stevens, Isaac Ingalls. *Report of Exploration of a Route for the Pacific Railroad, near the Forty-seventh and Forty-ninth Parallels, from St. Paul to Puget Sound.* Washington: n.p., 1855.

Sunder, John E. *The Fur Trade on the Upper Missouri, 1840–1865.* Norman: University of Oklahoma Press, 1965.

Tharpp, Dan L. *Encyclopedia of Frontier Biography.* 3 vols. Glendale: A. H. Clark, 1988.

Bibliography

Turner, Frederick. *Beyond Geography.* New York: Viking, 1980.

Turner, John Peter. *The North-West Mounted Police 1873–1893.* 2 vols. Ottawa: King's Printer, 1950.

U.S. Census, 1870. Montana.

Utley, Robert M. *The Indian Frontier of the American West, 1846–1890.* Albuquerque: University of New Mexico Press, 1984.

Utley, Robert M. *The Lance and the Shield.* New York: Henry Holt, 1993.

Van Kirk, Sylvia. *Many Tender Ties: Women in Fur Trade Society in Western Canada 1670–1870.* Winnipeg: Watson and Dwyer, 1980.

Waiser, William A. "The North-West Mounted Police in 1874–1889: A Statistical Study," Research Bulletin Number 117. Ottawa: Parks Canada, 1979.

Weeks, Mary L. *The Last Buffalo Hunter. As told to her by Norbert Welsh.* New York: Thomas Nelson & Sons, 1939.

Williams, Glyndwr. "The Hudson's Bay Company and the Fur Trade: 1670–1870." *The Beaver,* special ed., Autumn 1983, rpt. 1991.

Wilson, A., ed. *The Letters of Charles John Brydges, 1879–82.* Winnipeg: Hudson's Bay Record Society, 1979.

Wood, Jim, personal communication of August 9, 1992. Loma, Montana.

Newspapers

The *(Daily/Weekly) River Press,* Fort Benton, Montana.

The *Fort Benton Record,* Fort Benton, Montana.

The *Helena Daily Independent,* Helena, Montana.

The *Helena (Daily/Weekly) Herald,* Helena, Montana.

The *Kendall Miner,* Kendall, Montana.

The *Medicine Hat Daily News,* Medicine Hat, Alberta.

The *(Winnipeg) Standard,* Winnipeg, Manitoba.

INDEX

Cocking, Mathew, 25
Confederation, 31
Conrad, Charles, 44, 46
Conrad, William, 44, 46, 47
Cook, Caroline, 46
Coombs, Glorianna, 61
Coombs, Leonard Reed, 61
Coombs, Sarah, 61
Cowesses, 85, 108
Cowie, Isaac, 16, 38, 45, 46, 60
  and trading post, 41–42
Crazy Horse, 91, 92, 94
Cree, 63, 85, 86, 94, 101, 105, 110;
  alliance with Assiniboin, 31; alliance
  with Blackfoot, 31; and Big Bear, 109;
  and buffalo wars, 41; and changing
  economies, 30, 31, 32; and Cypress
  Hills Massacre, 66; and decline of
  buffalo, 28; and Home Farm Plan, 108;
  and Ottawa, 80, 87, 107; and reserves in
  Cypress Hills, 110; and trade, 38, 42,
  47; and Treaty 4, 106; and violence, 45;
  as danger in the Hills, 39; as middlemen
  in the fur trade, 29–30; as provisioners
  to the fur trade, 26; cycles of movement,
  81 (*see also* Plains Indians: cycles of
  movement); dependence on trade, 30;
  enemies of Dakota, 93, 97; independent
  of reserves, 109, 110; social structure
  of, 21, 31, 80–81; territory in 1700s, 21,
  25
Crook, George, 91, 92
Crooked Arm, 96
Crooked Lake, 106
Crow, 21, 31, 38, 47, 51, 61, 92, 94, 109
Crow's Dance, 96
Crozier, Supt. L. N. F., 103, 104
Culbertson, Alexander, 46
Cullen, W. E., 69
Curly (Crow scout), 92
Custer, Lt. Col. George A., 89, 90, 91, 92
Cypress Hills Massacre, 15, 47, 51, 52,
  59, 69, 70, 71, 72, 114
Cypress Hills, The: climate of, 17;
  geological history of, 17; vegetation of,
  18; wildlife in, 18, 41
Cypress Lake, 109

D

Dakota, 21, 25, 29, 38, 60, 62, 89, 98,
  99, 101; and gender studies, 33; and
  Nez Percé, 97–98; and Sitting Bull in
  Canadian territory, 88–105; and
  starvation, 94, 102, 103; and the War of
  1812, 89, 96; traditional territory of,
  89; U.S. missions for return of, 96, 98–
  101
Daniels (Métis scout), 95
Davis, D. W., 46
Day Star. *See* Kisecawchuck
De Courby, Father Jules, 40
Diehl, Charles, 99
Denomie, Xavier, 42
Dewdney, Edgar, 110
Dixons, The, 113
Downstream people, 85, 86, 87
Dumont, Gabriel, 104
Durfee and Peck, 43, 46, 60
Duval, John C., 65

E

Eagle Hills, 41
Earth Woman, 43
East End, 22, 47, 74, 94
Eastend, 19, 22
Elkwater Lake, 20, 22
English, John J., 108
Evans, John H., 47, 66, 68

F

Farwell, Abel, 38, 43, 46, 47, 48, 51, 62,
  63, 65, 66, 67, 68, 69; and wife, 61;
  description of, 59–61
Farwell's Post, 59, 60, 114; description of,
  60–61
Favel, John, Jr., 63
File Hills, 85
Fish Creek, 113
Fisk Wagon Road, 64
Flying Bird, 99
Foremost Man. *See* Nekaneet
Fort Battleford, 76
Fort Belknap, 92
Fort Benton, 61, 62, 63, 66, 78, 92; and
  mail, 47; and NWMP, 73, 76; as center of

Index

Q

Qu'Appelle Valley, 85, 106
Quesnell, Jules, 113

R

Rain-in-the-Face, 91
Ranching, 15, 112–14
Ray, Arthur, 80
RCMP, 113
Red Cloud (chief), 90, 91
Red Cloud Agency, 94
Red Deer River, 37
Red Ochre Hill, 85, 86
Red River, 22, 38, 39, 41, 44, 60, 108
Red River Resistance, 38
Reed, Hayter, 111
Regina, 76
Reno, Maj. Marcus A., 92
Reserves: and agriculture, 106, 107–09, 112; disallowed in Cypress Hills, 109–10; poverty on, 112; settlement of Indians on, 106–07; starvation on, 106, 107–08
Riel, Louis, 94, 101
Rivers, Paul, 47
Robbers Roost, 35
Rocky Mountain House, 42
Rondeau, Reverend Clovis, 39
Rosebud Creek, 91, 92
Round Lake, 106
Rowe, Charles, 62
Rowe, William, 47
Royal Irish Constabulary, 71

S

Sand Hills, 41
Sarsi, 20, 38, 94
Saulteaux, 21, 26, 85, 87, 88, 93, 94, 96, 106
Schultz, John Christian, 86
Sekani, 20
Setter, John, 108
Shoshoni, 31
Siksika, 20. See Blackfoot
Simpson, Sir George, 30
Sioux, 93, 103
Sisseton Dakota, 93

Sitting Bull, 92; and Fort Walsh, 76; and Louis Riel, 94; and NWMP, 94, 96; and resistance in U.S., 91–92, 94, 103; and Terry Commission, 99–101; and U.S. representatives, 96, 98–99; and Walsh, 95, 98, 99, 103, 104; death of, 104; in Canada, 95–105; origin of name, 89; persuaded to meet with Americans, 99; return to U.S., 104
Skull Creek, 113
Solomon, Esther, 64
Solomon, Gabriel, 95
Solomon, Moses, 38, 43, 47, 48, 63, 65, 66, 67, 68, 69; description of, 63–65
Solomon, Sol, 64
Solomon's Post, 59, 64, 114; description of, 65
South Saskatchewan River, 85
Spitzee Cavalry, 47, 62, 66
Spotted Eagle, 95, 99, 102
Spotted Tail, 94
St. Denis, Celistine, 113
St. Mary's River, 36, 60
Standoff Post, 35, 62
Star Child, 79
Stegner, Wallace, 79
Stillson, Jerome B., 99
Stobart, Eden and Co., 77
Stone, Jan, 99
Stoney. See Assiniboin
Storm Bear, 99
Strikes Plenty Woman, 61
Sun dance, 26, 81
Sun River, 36, 72
Swain, Francis Xavier, 113
Swan River Barracks, 72
Sweet Grass Hills, 47, 60, 87; massacre, 45, 66
Swift Current, 85
Swiftcurrent Creek, 85

T

T. C. Power and Co., 37, 43, 47, 48, 60, 62, 65, 77, 78
Tanner, John, 113
Tatanka-Tyotanka. See Sitting Bull
Taylor, Harry "Kamoose," 47
Ten Mile Coulee, 74

Terry, Alfred H., 74, 91, 92, 98, 99, 100, 101
Terry Commission, 98
Teton Dakota. *See* Dakota
Teton River, 44
The Crow, 99
The Gambler, 88, 106
The-Man-that-Scatters-the-Bear, 99
The-One-that-Runs-the-Ree, 100
Thirst dance. *See* Sun dance
Thunder Breeding Hills, 15
Titameg, 63
Tongue River Cantonment, 94
Touchwood Hills, 85
Touchwood People, 85
Traders, 22, 46; and competition, 47, 48, 49; and government contracts, 77–78; and violence, 40; arrival in fall, 28–29, 37; character of, 45, 46; forts, 28, 46, 50; licensing of, 43–44; routine, 47–48, 50–52; supplies, 48–49; transportation of goods, 49; wholesale, 44
Travois, 15, 17, 20, 27
Treaty 1, 86
Treaty 2, 86
Treaty 4, 85, 86, 87, 106, 109, 110
Treaty 6, 88, 107, 109
Tsuu T'ina. *See* Sarsi

U

Upstream people, 85

V

Val Marie, 113
Vision quests, 15, 74
Vogle, Philander, 63, 65

W

W. J. Wetzel 43
Walsh, Supt. James Morrow, 71, 72, 92, 114; and U.S. military, 102–03; relationship with Dakota, 93–105; removal, 103
Washita Valley, 90
Welsh, Norbert, 44–45
Whiskey trade, 15, 35, 41, 42, 43, 46, 52, 60, 62, 67, 71, 72, 76; and Act of Congress, 35; and Act of Parliament, 36; boosting traders' profits, 35–36

White Bird, 90, 98
White Calf, 86
White Dog, 95
White Eagle, 93
White Raven, 27
Whitemud River, 22, 38, 40, 95
Wildlife, 16
Wills, Alexander, 63
Wills, John, 63
Wills, John, Jr., 63
Wills, Rosalie, 63
Wincanahe, 67
Winter, 15, 17, 26, 27, 28, 37, 74, 81
Wolfers, 38, 40, 46, 47, 52, 62, 63; and Cypress Hills Massacre, 59, 66–70; and violence, 45
Wood and Anderson ranch, 114
Wood choppers, 61, 62, 64
Wood, David, 113
Wood Mountain, 39, 72, 97, 101; and Dakota, 93, 94, 97, 104; as subpost of Fort Walsh, 74, 93, 94, 95, 103; as wintering place for Indians, 86; Métis settlement at, 38, 39–40, 41

Y

Yellow Bull, 101
Yellow Dog, 99
Young Dogs, 85